# *BAD NEWS TRAVELS FAST*

Drawing by Norman, "Looking for Trouble," *Fourth Estate,* March 17, 1898. University of Minnesota Libraries.

–···/ ·–/ –··/ –·/ ·/ ·––/ ···/ –/ ·–·/ ·–/ ···–/ ·/ ·–··/ ···/ ··–·/ ·–/ ···/ –/

# *BAD NEWS TRAVELS FAST*

## *THE TELEGRAPH, LIBEL, AND PRESS FREEDOM IN THE PROGRESSIVE ERA*

*PATRICK C. FILE*

–···/ ·–/ –··/ –·/ ·/ ·––/ ···/ –/ ·–·/ ·–/ ···–/ ·/ ·–··/ ···/ ··–·/ ·–/ ···/ –/

*UNIVERSITY OF MASSACHUSETTS PRESS*
Amherst and Boston

Printed in the United States of America

ISBN 978-1-62534-374-1 (paper); 373-4 (hardcover)

Designed by Sally Nichols
Set in Arno Pro
Printed and bound by Maple Press, Inc.

Cover design by Thomas Eykemans

Library of Congress Cataloging-in-Publication Data
Names: File, Patrick C., author.
Title: Bad news travels fast : the telegraph, libel, and press freedom in the Progressive Era / Patrick C. File.
Description: Amherst : University of Massachusetts Press, 2019. | Based on author's thesis (doctoral)—University of Minnesota, 2013. | Includes bibliographical references and index. |
Identifiers: LCCN 2018019214 (print) | LCCN 2018031015 (ebook) | ISBN 9781613766200 (e-book) | ISBN 9781613766217 (e-book) | ISBN 9781625343741(pbk.) | ISBN 9781625343734 (hardcover)
Subjects: LCSH: Libel and slander—United States—History. | Trials (Libel)—United States—History. | Journalism—United States—History. | United States—History—1865–1921.
Classification: LCC KF1266 (ebook) | LCC KF1266 .F55 2019 (print) | DDC 345.73/0256—dc23
LC record available at https://lccn.loc.gov/2018019214

British Library Cataloguing-in-Publication Data
A catalog record for this book is available from the British Library.

Portions of this book are derived from two articles: Patrick C. File, "Retract, Expand: Libel Law, the Professionalization of Journalism, and the Limits of Press Freedom at the Turn of the Twentieth Century," *Communication Law and Policy* 22, no. 3 (2017): 275–308, copyright © Taylor & Francis, LLC, available at: https://doi-org.unr.idm.oclc.org/10.1080/10811680.2017.1331623; and Patrick C. File, "'Watchdog' Journalists and 'Shyster' Lawyers: Analyzing Legal Reform Discourse in the Journalistic Trade Press, 1895–1899," *American Journalism* 35, no. 3 (2018), copyright © Taylor & Francis, LLC. I thank the editors for their permission to use them here.

# *CONTENTS*

–·–·/–––/–·/–/·/–·/–/···/

# *PREFACE*

It can be surprising, invigorating, and a little troubling to look at the past and see reflections of the present. A mix of those reactions was the impetus to write this book and formulate its central argument about three little-known libel cases and the broader legal reform movement that surrounded them at the turn of the twentieth century. In *Bad News Travels Fast,* I argue that telegraph-driven libel cases spurred the press to articulate, debate, and litigate an important idea about freedom of the press in democratic society: that legal protection for the use of technology in gathering and disseminating newsworthy information was required if the press were to serve their crucial role in the public sphere.

I was surprised when I first encountered the libel cases of socialites Juliette Smith and Edward Rutherford, businessmen Tyndale Palmer and Joao Francisco de Freitas, and world famous entertainer Annie Oakley, because they had not been discussed extensively in my reading about legal challenges faced by the Progressive era press. I thought the scale and scope of the cases were noteworthy—the plaintiffs targeted hundreds of newspapers across the country between 1890 and 1910—and I thought it was interesting that they shared a common link to bad information spread fast and far by news wire services using the telegraph. Nevertheless, I found that almost no historical or legal writing made any reference to the cases as unique or interesting, let alone connected to each other. So I set out to uncover these stories and see what historical significance they might have.

It has been invigorating to find that Smith, Rutherford, Palmer, de Freitas, and Oakley are all characters who typified aspects of the American relationship with the press at the turn of the twentieth century, but whose experiences also resonate with relevance to today's media landscape. Smith and Rutherford, noteworthy for no reason other than their status as wealthy socialites, were victimized by the public's and press's fascination with the foibles of famous people. Palmer, an itinerant entrepreneur and businessman whose work life was in tune with the social and geographic mobility of the age, found himself accused of colluding with de Freitas in the kind of audacious international corporate corruption that would seem sadly familiar to news readers of the 1890s and today. Their response was to launch a sweeping legal crusade against the publishers who wronged them. Oakley was a trailblazing female entertainer—one of the first true international superstars—whose reliance on positive news coverage created an acrimonious legal fight when a dubious report of debauchery proved too tantalizing for the press to pass up.

The process of uncovering these stories was also troubling, however, as the deeper I dug into them the more I seemed to encounter a void in the broader scholarly conversation around the history and law of journalism and mass communication. As I searched for a conceptual framework to help explain what I was finding in the debate around these serial libel cases, I felt that much of the relevant scholarship in media history offered explanations for phenomena of the past that overlooked law or policy considerations, while the scholarship in media law that could help me contextualize the cases often discussed legal issues in ways that disregarded broader social or cultural factors. It seemed that shedding light on this fascinating set of libel cases offered an unexpected opportunity to make a meaningful contribution to answering overlapping historical and legal questions: How do we use law to define what makes an acceptable journalistic report? What role do evolving professional practices or the use of technology play in this important process?

My hope is that the resulting book reflects the surprising and vivid stories surrounding these cases and the crucial issues they raised, while making a serious scholarly intervention by bridging a gap in the way we think about the legal history of the American press. Readers should find invigorating familiarity in how the cases illustrate the tension that arises when competition to publish timely and entertaining content clashes with the social interest in preventing and compensating harm caused by sensationalism and inaccuracy. Readers might be troubled to find the cases reflect salient and unresolved challenges in balancing press freedom with responsibility and the risks and rewards of extending special legal privileges to the news media. I hope the book will prompt even more troubling and invigorating questions about the relationship between the press and the public in a vibrant democratic public sphere.

# ACKNOWLEDGMENTS

·–/–·–·/–·–/···/

I am grateful to consider the countless contributions, large and small, of numerous people in the writing of this book. I have been incredibly lucky to benefit from the thoughtful guidance of scholars whose roles in my ongoing development as a thinker and writer extend far beyond these pages. At the University of Minnesota, Professor Jane Kirtley has simply invested more time and energy in me and my scholarly work over the years since I became her advisee and mentee as a graduate student than I could ever repay. At various stages of this project, I have benefitted immensely from the enthusiastic and incisive counsel of Dr. Susanna Blumenthal and the kind and thoughtful encouragement of Dr. Barbara Welke, two legal historians whose challenging questions and important and innovative work have pushed me to be ambitious. Dr. Amy Kristin Sanders offered timely advice at pivotal early moments in the process, and I value her friendship. Dr. Kathy Roberts Forde has routinely dropped what she was doing to read what I'm working on, critique and help me contemplate, and offer heartfelt guidance and encouragement. Her warmth, grace, and intellectual verve are an inspiration. Dr. Brian Steffen has been a source of enthusiastic support on every step of my journey as a journalist, world-wanderer, and scholar since I showed up at Simpson College many years ago.

At the University of Massachusetts Press, executive editor Matt Becker has been unfailingly optimistic, thoughtful, and encouraging as he demystified the process of taking my proposal to a polished book, and he found excellent reviewers whose comments contributed mightily to the precision of the final product. I have also appreciated the patience, promptness, and professionalism of the entire production staff at the University of Massachusetts Press. Rudy Leon of Evoke: Words for Hire lent her editing expertise to formatting and a close reading of the manuscript, and I am grateful to her for that heavy lifting.

Where would we be without librarians? I am particularly indebted to George Jackson, Van Houlson, and Jan Nyberg at the University of Minnesota libraries, along with too many helpful experts to name at the American Antiquarian Society, Quinnipiac University, Simpson College, the University of Nevada, Las Vegas Boyd School of Law, and the University of Nevada, Reno.

More broadly, I have benefitted from the opportunity to study and teach alongside countless world class colleagues who may not even realize they made a contribution to the successful completion of this project. As a graduate student and later faculty member at the University of Minnesota School of Journalism and Mass Communication, I was the beneficiary of an endowment by the late Otto Silha and his family that supported my interest in media law and professional ethics. The friendships I have made at Minnesota, Simpson College, Quinnipiac University, University of St. Thomas, the University of Nevada, Reno's Reynolds School of Journalism and Center for Advanced Media Studies, and the conferences and colloquia of the Association for Education in Journalism and Mass Communication have helped sustain my long-term interest in answering challenging questions about the role journalism serves in democratic society.

For always encouraging me to ask challenging questions and being particularly tolerant as I exhaustively pursue the answers, I thank my parents, David and Patricia, and my sisters, Mary Kate and Erin. This book is dedicated to them.

*BAD*

*NEWS*

*TRAVELS*

*FAST*

# INTRODUCTION

··/–·/–/·–·/–––/

In August 1903, Annie Oakley was "at the bottom of the toboggan." So said the story that appeared in the Richmond, Virginia, *News Leader,* as well as in other newspapers across the United States: the world-famous sharpshooter had turned up in a Chicago courtroom, drug-addicted and destitute, accused of stealing a man's pants in order to buy cocaine. "The striking beauty of the woman, whom the crowds at the World's Fair admired, is gone," reported the *Scranton Truth.* The story, however, was false. The arrested woman turned out to be an imposter Oakley; one of at least two women who had toured the country claiming to be the famous entertainer and who, unlike the real Oakley, had fallen on hard times. The real Annie Oakley was vacationing in New Jersey at the time of the incident, having left Buffalo Bill Cody's Wild West Show a year earlier. Newspapers apologized for their mistakes and retracted the stories, but Oakley argued that the damage had already been done, so she set her sights on them, filing fifty-five libel lawsuits against newspapers across the country over the next seven years.[1]

Thus, Oakley joined the era's serial libel plaintiffs—a handful of people who sued numerous newspapers for republishing reports that were allegedly false and harmful to their reputations. The serial libel plaintiffs employed a long established legal action that could allow them to recover monetary damages in compensation for their harm, but they did so on a scale never seen before, suing newspapers in cities and towns that they might never have otherwise visited. The group included two socialites—Juliette Smith and Edward Rutherford—who sued newspapers in New York and Chicago for allegations of an illicit love affair, and two businessmen—Tyndale

Palmer and Joao Francisco de Freitas—who sued hundreds of newspapers across the country over a claim that they embezzled profits from the sale of a light bulb patent. Each of the serial libel cases arose because bad news could travel fast at the turn of the twentieth century. The news was bad for the plaintiffs and bad for the defendants: the stories were accidental falsehoods that could harm people's reputations while exposing publishers to legal liability. The news traveled fast: electric telegraph lines carried it almost instantly from trusted wire services like the Associated Press and United Press Association to newsrooms across the country where it hastily went into print—usually without independent verification—as a routine and integral part of the business of publishing the news.

This book explains how law, technology, and evolving ideas about press freedom, reputation, and privacy intertwined in these fascinating cases, highlighting tension in the press's relationship with the public, challenging the press's professional identity, and influencing a pivotal debate about journalism in a democratic society. The cases tested the limits of libel law, raising novel questions: whether courts should account for the fact that the libelous reports originated with wire services, whether plaintiffs' compensation should be limited when they sued numerous publishers using the same libel claim, and whether the harm done by libel could be diluted by the distance and decentralization afforded by a high-speed information-sharing network. In placing these questions before judges and juries that sometimes viewed the press as careless and freewheeling, the cases helped push a broader debate about the rights and responsibilities of the American press out of newsrooms and press club parlors and into courtrooms and legislative chambers. Discourse surrounding the cases—in court, in news coverage, in commentary, and in the lobbying efforts of professional journalists' associations—linked mass communication technology to a key problem that continues to challenge scholars today: whether the U.S. Constitution's guarantee of "freedom of the press" requires special legal privileges for the news media, beyond those extended to all speakers.

I argue that in the serial libel cases, the press began to tie a commercial imperative to a legal one: claiming that the use of technology in gathering and disseminating information quickly and efficiently required strong legal protection for newspapers' social role in the democratic public sphere. The cases were crucial in shaping the legal consciousness surrounding libel law—and ultimately, press freedom—at a pivotal historical moment of evolving professional identity. Ultimately, these largely forgotten cases are important because they influenced how Americans think about the democratic concept of press freedom, and because they raised legal and social issues that are familiar today, illustrating the tension that arises when competition to meet the public appetite for timely and entertaining content clashes with the interest in preventing and compensating harm caused by sensationalism and inaccuracy.

At the turn of the twentieth century, newspapers depended on a vast telecommunication network to meet the public's demand for information. The telegraph had been a pervasive part of the American newspaper industry since the 1850s.[2] Its speed and scale made it the most powerful information distribution network ever created, but those qualities also amplified legal risks associated with spreading false stories of debauchery and corruption through the news. By the late 1800s, Americans were more mobile—geographically and socially—than ever before in history, and concerns about privacy and reputation became increasingly acute.[3] People worried about whether nearby neighbors or distant strangers saw them as chaste, honest, and virtuous, and the law reflected those concerns.

Meanwhile, the legal doctrine of libel—which allows individuals to sue for damages when their reputations are harmed by false utterances, publications, or republications—did not favor the press. In politics, libel served to protect "the best men" from mean-spirited attacks that could drive them out of public service.[4] In cases involving nonpublic, nonpolitical individuals, court decisions tended to maintain a tenuous balance of respectability among the classes and were generally considered a means to offer correction and compensation to those unsettled or offended by the sudden spotlight of public scrutiny.[5] Indeed, libel suits could provide Victorian era women a sliver of independence amid a growing struggle for equality.[6] Courts that heard libel cases were chiefly concerned with preventing impertinent speech and protecting personal reputation rights; the law did not yet recognize defenses that could limit news media liability for republishing wire service content,[7] and the U.S. Supreme Court would not consider the First Amendment implications of punishing libelous speech until the landmark 1964 case *New York Times v. Sullivan.*[8] Instead, at the turn of the twentieth century, mistakes and misjudgments—including republishing erroneous wire service stories—could subject newspaper editors and publishers to almost automatic liability. "Tale-bearers are as bad as tale-makers" was the adage repeated in court opinions and legal treatises.[9] As false and harmful tales were borne almost instantly along the news industry's telegraph lines and through the wire services, the potential for harm—to the stories' unwitting subjects and to all the newspapers that published them—was made manifest through serial libel cases.

In telling the story of the serial libel cases, *Bad News Travels Fast* draws together formative concepts from the cultural history of journalism and critical legal history: communication historian James Carey's notion of the "idea of a report," which he considered the focal point of an ongoing social negotiation of acceptable journalistic forms and practices for "rendering reality," and legal historian Robert Gordon's view of law as an indeterminate and socially contingent process through which conflicting ideas are mediated.[10] For Carey, because the journalistic report is a form of cultural expression that reflects journalists' interpretation of reality, the thinking around it is an important subject of study as an evolving, socially contingent, and influential "expression of human consciousness."[11] The connection between the journalistic report and consciousness fits into Carey's broader cultural historical argument that communication should be viewed as a "ritual . . . directed not toward the extension of messages in space but toward the maintenance of society in time."[12] For journalism and communication scholars, Carey's concept of consciousness has proven both compelling and ambiguous. Although the concept has led to a better historical understanding of the social role of journalism by taking in a broad view of the discourse surrounding reporting, the concept has not offered much toward an overall understanding of the history of consciousness.[13] "Legal consciousness," meanwhile, has become a key concept in the critical legal historical project of explaining how dominant legal ideologies are formulated, ingrained, challenged, and changed, through both formal and informal arenas of law, by studying how law is experienced and understood in society. As with Carey's use of the concept of consciousness, while "legal consciousness" has sometimes suffered from a lack of conceptual clarity or consistency, it has nevertheless helped illuminate a path toward a clearer understanding of how society uses law to mediate among contradicting ideas about order, organization, power, and equality.[14]

These concepts converge over the fundamental notion that both journalism and law are important social structures that are themselves created and maintained by democratic society. Both consist of institutions and paradigms of thought that are subject to social negotiation, and neither is autonomous nor insulated from influence by external individuals or groups. The legal questions that the serial libel cases raised were also questions at the heart of the social negotiation of the idea of a report at the turn of the twentieth century: whether the public interest was served by the widespread publication of people's personal affairs, whether the economic interests served by sensationalism justified inclusion in the news, and whether the publication of falsehoods should be permitted, or should be forgiven when the publication was accidental.

The interdisciplinary conceptual framework employed here can help us understand the serial libel cases as an important historical moment when contradictory ideas about journalism's social role and professional practices clashed in courts of law as well as in the court of public opinion. It encourages us to examine the discourse surrounding the cases—in court opinions, legal treatises, lobbying strategies, and journalistic coverage and commentary—to discover and assess how these ideas were formulated, articulated, and contested in the public sphere.

Although the idea of a report as a reflection of social consciousness has drawn sustained interest and investigation among journalism and communication historians, few of those studies have incorporated law or legal consciousness. Studies of media law in history, on the other hand, have tended to focus on the sources of intellectual history of freedom of speech while mostly neglecting professional practices and standards of journalism as an important factor in legal consciousness. Bringing legal perspectives into the discussion of the cultural history of journalism can expand our understanding of journalism history by drawing important processes of social negotiation and definition into the picture, building a strong connection between two disciplines, and providing a more comprehensive view of the development of journalism as a reflection of social consciousness. This book aims to demonstrate the value of such an interdisciplinary approach to legal history in journalism and mass communication by exploring ideas about press freedom and journalistic professionalism in the discourse surrounding the serial libel cases.

We can see the serial libel cases as a formative moment in a long-running and ongoing debate about the purposes and limits of the First Amendment. This book joins an active historical project aimed at uncovering the "forgotten years" of free expression—a period during the late nineteenth and early twentieth century when courts rarely offered direct or explicit interpretations of the fundamental speech rights enshrined in the First Amendment or state constitutions, but when important thinking about free speech was nonetheless prevalent in various legal conflicts and in Americans' daily discourse.[15] In addition to explaining how legal disputes helped delimit speech and behavior in the public sphere at this time, scholars have shown how some legal threats—like an increase in libel suits and the prosecution of a reporter who refused to reveal a confidential source—led the press to frame itself as a unique and important institution requiring special legal protections.[16] This is a view that continues to be contested as a matter of legal and political philosophy: should the First Amendment's clause that forbids government abridgement of "freedom of the press" protect all speakers who use technology to publish information, or should it extend special privileges to a particular institution—"the press"—that serves the public interest? This debate has been revived and reenergized as digital technologies have placed the tools of instant global information dissemination in the hands of every Internet user.[17]

The story told here can add important historical context to this debate, toward a better understanding of how technological and professional changes in the American press have influenced legal consciousness surrounding the purpose of the press clause. The libel cases at the center of this story became serial libel cases because of the telegraph—a high-speed communication technology that had become indispensable to the news business in spite of the risk it created for systematically spreading false and harmful news far and wide. In fighting these cases and raising the alarm over the broader threat they posed, the press began to blend together economic and philosophical justifications for their role in democratic society, arguing that their use of the valuable technology of the telegraph must be protected because its social benefits outweighed its risks. The cases therefore offer a unique opportunity to consider the promise and peril of such technology in news media and its role in the legal consciousness of press freedom alongside other, more traditional concerns about lawsuits causing chilling effects and inhibiting the press's role in public transparency and accountability.

The serial libel cases can also help us better understand the role technology played in the social construction of the idea of a report through evolving values and practices of journalism at the turn of the twentieth century. Scholars who have studied the rise of new communication technologies have explained how their historical significance becomes clear not at the moment of invention, but rather when they are institutionalized—as their socially acceptable uses are negotiated and renegotiated.[18] This book places the use of the telegraph and the legal consciousness surrounding it within the context of a key period in the professional development of journalism. At the turn of the twentieth century, the press's goals and values were widely debated in the public sphere amid new social concerns about privacy, reputation, and sensationalism. Scholars have depicted an era of tension between "two hallowed principles, a right to know and a right to be left alone"[19] and shown how publishers hotly debated competing approaches to telling stories that sold newspapers, from detached and fact-based methods to more activist and flamboyant styles associated with "yellow journalism."[20] Others have described how the telegraph and wire service news helped change nearly everything about the modus operandi of American newspapers in the late nineteenth century, from reporters' writing style to the very structure of the business.[21] Through its account of the serial libel cases, this book draws together these strands of scholarship, showing how values of speed and scale collided with emerging concerns about scandals-as-news and the need to protect personal reputation in an expanding public sphere. By considering what certain individuals and groups considered to be the best "report" as a means to reflect and construct reality, how that idea was contested, and by whom, the book offers a better understanding of the social role that people expected those forms, practices, and technologies of journalism to play. Thus, the crux of the book's interdisciplinary historical approach is a more holistic view of the relationship between the press's professional values, technology, and social conceptions of press freedom.

The book tells the story of the serial libel cases in three parts. The first two chapters lay out the context and background for the cases. They explain how newspapers' social and civic role evolved during the late nineteenth century through debates about professionalism and propriety, how the telegraph and wire services helped to introduce industrialized speed and scale to the newspaper business while creating tension with emerging professional values like public service and accuracy, and how judges rethought the concepts of fault and liability amid an industrializing and accident-prone society but resisted applying that paradigm shift to the law of libel. The middle three chapters recount the serial libel cases in chronological order: first the Smith and Rutherford cases between 1890 and 1898, then the Palmer and de Freitas cases between 1892 and 1902, and finally the Oakley cases, from 1903 to 1907. The last three chapters assess the press's response to the cases in courts and in legislatures, and offer some conclusions. While newspapers saw meager success in asking appellate judges for lenience in the form of special defenses in the serial libel suits, their professional associations achieved moderate success in seeking state laws that offer protection or privilege in some instances of erroneous libel.

The historical account that follows provides sorely needed context for today's debates about the relationship between mass communication technology and public discourse. Ultimately, I hope to provide a framework for better understanding the challenges facing publishers and lawmakers in today's media landscape, where new platforms for free expression can breed uncivil discourse, defamation, harassment, and invasions of personal privacy. More than a captivating set of legal stories that elucidate the interconnected history of technology, law, and press freedom in America, the serial libel cases offer an opportunity for an in-depth case study of how society uses law to define and delineate the role of journalism in American democracy: to confront problems accompanying the use of technology, to assess evolving professional standards, and to weigh competing ideas about the purpose of press freedom.

# CHAPTER 1

# *NEWS IN THE LATE NINETEENTH CENTURY*

–·/·/·––/···/

## MORE AND FASTER

The stories that led Juliette Smith, Edward Rutherford, Tyndale Palmer, Joao Francisco de Freitas, and Annie Oakley to launch their nationwide libel campaigns were altogether typical of American newspapers at the turn of the twentieth century. On any day of any week, one could pick up a copy of the local paper and read about scandalous love affairs, shady business deals, or petty crime, alongside news of politics and government. Journalism in the 1890s and 1900s was a product of intertwining changes: the newspaper industry had steadily expanded and incorporated faster communications technology while its role in society had evolved in response to competitive pressures for ever-fresher and more interesting news. The serial libel suits emerged as these changes came into tension with the social values of personal reputation and privacy. At the core of this tension were complex questions about the idea of a report and the role of newspapers in the public sphere: What information should be public and why? How should speed and accuracy be balanced in the competitive news business?

Debate over these questions occurred against a broader backdrop of concern about a loss of control over personal information. As nineteenth-century revolutions in transportation and communication connected countryside towns to each other and to larger cities along postal roads, rail lines, telegraph and telephone lines, Americans became more geographically and socially mobile. Millions of immigrants poured into the country, while millions more—especially the white men who most benefitted from the promise of American liberty—moved around in search of better work, better lives, and social status in frontier towns and growing cities. In a modernizing and merit-based society, greater mobility required greater wariness of the value of one's reputation, as it could both precede and follow you. Among all classes, but particularly the middle and upper classes, the extent to which a man was seen as trustworthy often translated directly to his ability to get a job or be extended credit, especially in unfamiliar circumstances; the extent to which a woman was considered chaste or virtuous had tremendous value in a society where her role was usually limited to tending to home and family.[1]

As early as 1838, writer James Fenimore Cooper complained of the way the modern press "tyrannizes over publick men, letters, the arts, the stage, and even over private life."[2] Cooper had personal reasons to challenge changing journalistic values: between 1837 and 1843 he initiated numerous libel suits against newspaper editors who criticized his work.[3] But his personal concerns reflect broader unease about an increasingly powerful industry focused on publicizing and criticizing personal moral lapses as much as public crime and corruption. In the 1830s, publishers learned that they could make more money selling advertising in cheap, widely circulated newspapers than through the traditional subscription model. Advertising revenue—tied to a growing consumer culture—was circulation-driven, so news was tailored to maximize broad public interest. The news that was easiest to gather and sell was easily readable content that included timely tidbits of local news as well as stories that appealed to readers' "human interest" such as crime, sex, scandal, corruption, and poverty—sometimes with a loose association to truth or accuracy. The lifestyles of the rich and famous as well as the poor and overlooked were dramatized and commodified. High-speed presses, running first on steam and then electricity, churned out more news on ever-cheaper paper to reach a growing, diversifying, and increasingly literate American public in the industrial cities of the East, Northeast, and Midwest. Between the 1830s and the 1890s, news publishing became a large and profitable American business thanks to this new "popular press" model, relying on industrialized innovation and efficiency to develop and deliver its product to thousands of daily readers.[4]

A social debate about an acceptable journalistic report arose with the press's changing focus and sense of professional purpose at the turn of the twentieth century, with concerns about privacy, propriety, and reputation at its center. The press's quest for interesting, important, and popular stories for consumer gratification and public service directly conflicted with Victorian values that prized reticence, good manners, and a veneer of respectability among the upper classes. Moralists, scholars, lawmakers, and journalists considered how to define and protect the rights and interests of individuals, the public, and the press, while balancing the public's right to know and an individual's right to be left alone. Those who favored greater restraint argued that the excesses of the popular press debased society, threatened domestic tranquility, and unjustly usurped the right to retain control of personal information.[5] In 1890, attorneys Samuel Warren and Louis Brandeis called for a new, more robust "right to privacy" in the *Harvard Law Review,* in an article aimed squarely at a press that was "overstepping in every direction the obvious bounds of propriety and of decency."[6] Publishers and press advocates, meanwhile, claimed that their expansion into the private sphere served an allegiance to public service, morality, and social reform. Newspapers raised public standards, they argued, when they exposed the lowest of the low and upheld the tradition of a free press in a democratic society. They were "the remorseless prosecution, defense, and judge in a court of public opinion."[7] Such an expansive and proactive idea of a journalistic rendering of reality offended high society, which would have preferred that the press—and its idea of a report—focus on praising the good rather than exposing the bad.

By the late 1890s, the exposure approach to a journalistic report had largely won out, and American newspaper publishers were engaged in what one press historian has called a "clash of paradigms" among competing approaches to telling and selling news stories, exemplified by three of the most popular New York City papers.[8] A "detached, impartial, fact-based" approach was led by the *New York Times* under its new motto, "All the News That's Fit to Print." A more activist and flamboyant approach, widely derided as "yellow journalism," was extolled and perfected by the *New York Journal*'s William Randolph Hearst. A narrative, literary approach was pioneered by Lincoln Steffens as editor of the *New York Commercial Advertiser.* The different approaches not only represented competing journalistic forms and practices, but also various sides of a developing journalistic identity, built on the public-service ethic that emerged as newspapers became politically independent beginning in the mid-nineteenth century but also reflecting progressive and reform ideals of social responsibility and scientific methodology.[9]

The ethical debate in the press was also driven by hallmarks of professionalization that emerged in the late nineteenth century: professional organizations and trade publications. Press associations emerged and flourished as a unique part of a broader movement toward professional organization in the United States in the late nineteenth century.[10] As communities became less isolated and more commercially consolidated, journalists sought to collaborate, discuss, and develop their industry with a spirit of common purpose and duty. The first national press association, the National Editorial Association, was founded in 1885, building on the city, state, and regional groups that emerged and thrived from the middle of the nineteenth century. According to NEA founder and first president Benjamin B. Herbert, the "social and educational" group aimed to "broaden the views of the members of the profession," drawing delegates from state press associations and holding annual meetings in different scenic locales each year.[11] Two years later came the American Newspaper Publishers Association, composed of publishers and business managers for daily newspapers in cities across the country. The group met annually in New York City, focusing primarily on the business interests of its members. The International League of Press Clubs was founded in 1891 and included more than forty press clubs across the country. A notable feature of the ILPC was that both men and women were welcome as members and leaders.[12] Although the national press associations varied in membership and focus, they shared an interest in defining their professional identity as a matter of both pride and profitability, playing a key structural role in establishing acceptable journalistic forms and practices that constituted a journalistic report. Ideals of public service, accuracy, and trustworthiness were at the heart of attempts to shed old images as partisan, scandal-mongering drunkards.[13]

Journalists' trade publications also emerged in the 1880s and 1890s as part of the press's nascent push for professionalization. Weekly or monthly periodicals like the *Journalist, Newspaperdom, Fourth Estate,* and *Editor and Publisher* offered a forum for the discussion and formation of ethical standards, although they could be infrequent and ideologically inconsistent.[14] For example, the front page of the April 9, 1896, edition of *Newspaperdom* featured a reprint of a *Scribner's* magazine essay by Aline Gorren entitled "Ethics of Modern Journalism." Gorren argued that the press failed to provide Americans with the vital information needed to live and thrive in a complex world full of equal opportunity, being obsessed with "various forms of personal gossip" and falsely promoting the idea that "in publicity, [there is] . . . enormous power for compelling righteousness."[15] In a response on page six of the same issue, *Newspaperdom*'s editors criticized Gorren's essay as "a curious jumble of chaotic suggestions," and called her view of the press "rather stale" and "overworked."[16]

A few weeks later, however, *Newspaperdom* editors hailed an essay criticizing "muck-rake journalism" as "a strong arraignment of a too common type of newspaper." The essay, originally published in the *St. Louis Observer,* argued that "every decent man and woman knows that there are some subjects which are never discussed in respectable society," and that "the newspaper claims the right to be nasty, and still be regarded as decent and respectable," even as editors and publishers "take up street gossip and fling it to the winds, all for the sake of gratifying the vitiated taste which they themselves have created and cultivated." Such journalism "can put up no excuse for its sins that will bear the test of reason and sound morality."[17] Ten years later, President Theodore Roosevelt more famously adopted the term "muckrake" in a 1906 speech comparing reform-minded investigative journalism to "the man with the muck rake" in John Bunyan's seventeenth-century novel *Pilgrim's Progress.*[18]

Overall, historians have argued that the journalism trade press's attention to ethical concerns tended to increase following noteworthy and controversial incidents, such as the exhaustive and intrusive coverage of President Grover Cleveland and his new wife, Frances Folsom, on their honeymoon in 1886 or the appearance of Warren and Brandeis's "right to privacy" article in 1890, and that their coverage became more sophisticated and consistent as journalists' views on ethics and professionalism became more standardized in the early twentieth century.[19]

The tension between professionalism and profit in the popular press was also heightened by the challenges of a fast-paced industrialized business environment. Revolutions in communications technology helped drive massive growth and structural change in the newspaper industry. Between 1830 and 1909, the number of daily newspapers published in the United States rose from 65 to 2,600, while the average circulation for those dailies rose from 2,986 to 9,312. In 1850, 4.6 percent of Americans subscribed to a daily newspaper; by 1930 it was 43.1 percent. Newspapers expanded westward along with the population.[20] Meanwhile, the typical urban newspaper grew from a relatively small operation run by an editor and a few assistants into a large and complex business. Newsrooms, pressrooms, advertising, distribution, and business operations became specialized and departmentalized, especially in the decades following the Civil War. The newsrooms of large metropolitan newspapers moved from an organizational structure that centered around a multipurpose editor to a structure that utilized several editors leading different sections, headed by a publisher focused on the overarching business concerns of the enterprise. Before the era of the popular press, a single editor or publisher could typically be expected to know what was on every page of his or her newspaper, and was often intimately involved with most of what was published. By the 1890s, however, journalists argued that the expansion, segmentation, and speed of the average newsroom made such awareness impractical if not impossible for a single editor.[21] Thus, the demand for speed and scale created an increasingly complex and diffuse chain of accountability when problems arose.

The organizational revolution in the news industry was part of a broader trend in American business in the late 1800s—explosive growth, professionalization, and the integration of production, distribution, and marketing—that had important implications for the social role of industry.[22] The growth and segmentation of management of the typical newspaper complicated the process of publishing news as well as the definition of success for the enterprise. Advertising departments measured success by the amount of space sold for ads, circulation departments by the timely delivery of papers to as many readers as possible, and editorial departments by the accuracy of news, its timeliness, and its relevance to readers. At times these differing definitions were at cross-purposes, like when a late-breaking news event delayed production and distribution.[23]

Technology—and particularly the electric telegraph—played a pivotal role in the ability of the popular press to reach a wider audience, and to do so with greater speed, meeting ever-increasing competitive demands for faster, fresher news. Newspapers had used cooperatives and joint ventures to gather and share news long before telegraphic technology existed, relying on everything from fast boats to express trains and even carrier pigeons.[24] The U.S. postal service had offered newspapers the cheapest and most efficient communication network in the world since 1792. Using free "exchanges," editors and publishers could collect news from all over the country for dissemination via their own newspapers.[25] However, with the advent and diffusion of the telegraph, which could transmit messages almost instantly by electrical signal using a simple code language, long-distance communication no longer relied on physical transportation. The New York Associated Press (later to become the powerful Associated Press) first put the telegraph to use for sharing news in 1848, and it grew to widespread use for that purpose as wires spread across the country and newspapers joined wire services in the following decades.[26]

The telegraph and wire services helped drive timeliness to the top of the list of professional journalism's values in the late nineteenth century. It shaped the idea of a report, in the form of newsgathering practices and public expectations of news content, as much as other professional standards. As news was gathered and delivered in smaller, more frequent updates, readers experienced greater urgency in following a story as it developed, and greater satisfaction in the speed with which they found out about it.[27] Wire services also contributed to the idea of a report by moving the style away from lyrical, narrative news writing and toward an "inverted pyramid" form (short, declarative, factual statements delivered in descending order of importance), an innovation linked to necessity due to occasionally unreliable equipment. Political neutrality was favored, as it made the news more palatable to publishers and readers across the political spectrum.[28] The telegraph-based wire service network standardized the presentation and diffusion of American news in a way that meant that readers of the *Winona* (Minnesota) *Republican* and the Keokuk, Iowa, *Constitution* could expect to read much of the same news, in virtually the same form, at virtually the same time, as readers in New York, Cincinnati, and San Francisco.[29]

Standardization and nationalization had a significant downside, however, in enabling flawed news to spread throughout the network as quickly as accurate news. The problems confounded politicians in the mid-1800s enough that they began releasing transcripts of speeches to the media prior to their public delivery in order to prevent the process of transcription and transmission from mangling their words and policy positions when they appeared in the newspaper.[30] Facing pressure to deliver messages faster and more cheaply (when telegraph services charged by the letter), many news wire operators devised codes and abbreviations, which could lead to confusion and inaccuracy in news reports delivered via telegraph.[31] At an institutional level, journalism confronted the prospect of compromising accuracy in the interests of speed and scale. Reporters felt immense competitive pressure to deliver news that was both timely and accurate, making mistakes feel inevitable. "The manager's chief difficulty," wrote an editor for the *New York Commercial Advertiser* in 1895, "is protecting his readers and public generally . . . [from] unavoidable errors."[32]

Complicated corporate structures, the heat of competition, and a reluctance to question wire services' original reports combined to make bad news travel fast. In its defense against a libel case in 1894, the *New York World* placed the blame for a false report on one of the paper's wire service editors. The Second Circuit U.S. Court of Appeals recounted the *World*'s description of its practices:

> The function of the telegraph editor is to read over carefully any dispatch received by him, to correct the English, to eliminate anything which he thinks does any injustice to anybody or anything, or which causes a doubt in the mind of the reader as to the accuracy of the dispatch, and to put headlines on. Thereupon the dispatch is sent to the composing room, and in due course is printed in the paper. The "publisher" of the *World* testified that the authorized custom in its office is that, unless a dispatch from a distant city "*per se* raises in the mind of the telegraph editor a suspicion of its accuracy, then he cannot change the facts; and it is optional with him then to judge of the importance of the dispatch, and withhold it from the composing room or have it set up." Where there is nothing on the face of the dispatch which raises a natural doubt as to its accuracy, it goes to the composing room, with its statement of facts substantially unchanged.[33]

The *World* explained that the dispatch in question in the case, sent from Cincinnati, differed significantly from the libelous story that ran in the newspaper, but it could not explain where in the process the alteration occurred, because "the dispatch as written out by the telegraph employee in the *World* office could not be found, nor [could the *World*] show which one of its 10 telegraph editors had received it." The court noted that the *World*'s practices "required no effort to be made to verify the accuracy of such dispatches, and no such effort was made in this instance."[34]

The *Cincinnati Post,* in defending itself against one of Annie Oakley's lawsuits in 1905, conceded that competition played a role in its publication of the false story about her, in a stark illustration of the way the idea of a report could combine conflicting news values that prized both scandal and speed. The *Post*'s telegraph editor testified that he included the story about Oakley's arrest and drug addiction shortly after he received it from the Scripps-McRae Press Association because it "was an interesting news item because of the celebrity of the person involved." It was not the editor's typical practice to check facts from wire services, and "it was published immediately, for fear of a 'scoop' by some rival."[35]

In an industry where a reputation for distributing faulty news could drive down wire service membership or subscription numbers, wire services also rejected blame for errors and inaccuracies along the murky chain of causation. In 1896, United Press filed a $5,000 libel suit against the Rochester, New York, *Herald* after the newspaper claimed a dispatch sent out by the UP was a "willful falsification."[36] In December 1899, a claim by the trade journal *Newspaperdom* that the American Press Association frequently exposed its subscribers to legal problems drew an angry rebuke from the company's president. In his letter to *Newspaperdom*'s editor, APA president O. J. Smith claimed that "only three times in eighteen years . . . have any of our customers been even threatened with suit for a libel contained in our matter." *Newspaperdom*'s claims of inaccuracy could not possibly be justified, Smith wrote, when "putting the few mistakes which can be charged to us against all of the possibilities of errors in the complicated nature and great variety of matter supplied by us." The APA might not be perfect, Smith argued, but it was very good, and it would be difficult in the complex industry to identify the source of any particular error anyway.[37]

As the popular press's business model increasingly relied on a combination of sensationalism and speed to drive circulation throughout the late nineteenth century, the risk of accidents—in the form of errors and inaccuracies—also increased, and with it the likelihood of libel suits. For nearly fifty years leading up to the 1890s, the telegraph had played an integral role in developing journalistic values of speed and scale in news gathering and publishing, and the telegraph-based wire services had helped incorporate those values into the idea of a report reflected by the practices of publishers and journalists and the expectations of readers. By the turn of the twentieth century, it was clear that newer technologies like wireless telegraphy, telephones, and hot metal typesetting would keep industry pressure and public expectations high for more news delivered across greater distances with greater timeliness.[38] In the serial libel cases, those journalistic values collided with emerging concerns about the propriety of rendering a reality that treated scandals as news and the need to protect personal reputation in an expanding public sphere. The cases would strain the limits of libel law by raising tough questions about the role of technology in press freedom and the legal parameters of accountability.

CHAPTER 2

# *LIBEL IN THE NINETEENTH CENTURY*

·–··/··/–···/·/·–··/

## MALICE OR MISTAKES?

Editors and publishers who were engaged in the complex and competitive process of publishing news in the late nineteenth century faced a legal atmosphere that was intolerant of bad news that traveled fast. The law disfavored publishers who claimed to have accidentally or unknowingly published news reports that were false and harmful to a plaintiff's reputation. Such circumstances did not offer the traditional defenses for true statements or narrow privileges protecting political criticism. Moreover, republishing or repeating a false, harmful story was considered just as bad as the original publication. Judges repeated the adage that "tale-bearers are as bad as tale-makers."[1] At the same time, however, the industrialization of American society was forcing jurists to rethink the concepts of fault and liability all across tort law. The news industry's modern processes and practices raised questions that complicated the traditional legal analysis and challenged the conventional legal consciousness surrounding libel and freedom of the press: Should inaccurate reports that are published by accident be treated the same as intentional or malicious lies, and should each republication of those reports be treated the same as the original publication? How should the law define the relative rights and responsibilities of the press and plaintiffs as technology plays a larger role in the process of publishing news?

Defendant publishers claimed they could not have intended to harm plaintiffs, because they had never met or heard of them, or claimed ignorance that allegedly libelous statements were published in the first place. Sometimes editors and reporters claimed that allegedly libelous reports came from individuals, newspapers, or news wires that they relied on regularly and considered trustworthy. As newspapers' business models increased the speed, scale, and scope of news, judges, juries, and journalists played integral roles in negotiating the idea of a report and setting the boundary lines of press freedom.

Newspaper editors and publishers complained loudly that libel suits had become too common and the law offered them too little protection. Contemporary reports from the late 1800s and scholarly research on that period show a surge in libel suits in the decades following the Civil War, owing to professional changes in the fields of journalism as well as law. One 1869 survey found 700 recent suits with damage claims totaling almost $50 million.[2] An 1895 editorial in the *Journalist* reflected the perception of an imbalance of justice in the legal consciousness surrounding libel: "Libel laws simply offer a premium to pettifogging attorneys, who shower vexatious litigation upon newspapers at enormous cost to the publishers, and not one in ten is proved to be justified if the case ever reaches trial. In a vast majority of instances the whole purpose of such actions is to blackmail publishers, and chiefly for the benefit of shysters rather than to do justice to injured citizens."[3]

There was some truth in the trade paper's bluster. Editors were at least partially right to blame speculative attorneys using the new innovation of a contingency fee—an agreement by which a lawyer took nothing if a suit was lost but a large sum if it was won—to encourage potential libel plaintiffs to target the press.[4] The legal profession in general experienced a boom after the Civil War, and "increased competition for business," wrote one legal historian, "appears to have pushed the newcomers at the bar . . . to generate new kinds of business."[5] On the other hand, urban dailies' scandal-mongering and sensationalism, when combined with the complex and mistake-prone processes of high-speed newsgathering and publishing, also contributed to the surge in libel suits.[6]

In the meantime, some newspapers even tried extralegal means of discouraging libel suits. Editors in Detroit, Boston, and Cincinnati each formed agreements not to publish stories about libel suits in their cities, hoping to lower public awareness and cut down on the suits. The conspiracy of silence was thought to diminish the overall frequency of nuisance suits, and they recommended it to papers in other cities.[7] However, Milton McRae of the *Cincinnati Post* and *St. Louis Chronicle* warned that any such agreement should be tacit and not written down. McRae said the Cincinnati papers' agreement—which had been documented—was exposed in an 1893 libel case against the *Post,* and he thought it led the jury to award a larger verdict against the newspaper as it was used as evidence of malice.[8] In 1898 the New York Press Association offered a $5,000 reward "for proof against lawyers who have excited groundless actions or legal proceedings against any daily newspaper" in New York. The idea was that potential plaintiffs would opt for the guaranteed $5,000 when approached by "shysters" who offered to represent them on a contingent basis in a libel suit, rather than go to court and risk losing.[9] These creative approaches to confronting the problem that publishers saw in libel, along with the claims that lawyers and plaintiffs set out to "blackmail" newspapers, suggest the extent to which the legal consciousness surrounding the issue involved considerations of economics as much as it did simple justice or providing proper compensation for a wrong.

Overall, crippling damage awards were relatively rare, but fighting or settling the suits could be very expensive.[10] The *Vindicator* of Youngstown, Ohio, reported that it was the target of ten libel suits between 1893 and 1897, with claims totaling $250,000. "The total verdicts rendered against this paper in all these suits amounted to just one dollar and one cent—and all have been paid in full," the *Vindicator* reported.[11] Larger papers hired in-house lawyers to provide regular counsel and pre-publication review.[12] In 1888, the *Philadelphia Times* expressed growing frustration: "The average cost of defending a libel suit, including the necessary time, preparation, employment of counsel, etc., is about $500. . . . The Times has paid over $20,000 for the defence [*sic*] of libel suits since it was founded thirteen years ago, and there is a judgment or an acquittal in every case. In other words, this journal has paid over $20,000 as the price of exposing wrong-doers and battling foolish suitors or worse than foolish lawyers to maintain the freedom of the press in the most liberal civilization of the world."[13]

The manager of the *Denver Republican* complained to the American Newspaper Publishers Association in 1895 that a single libel case that reached the state Supreme Court three times had ended in a modest verdict for $650, but "I paid about $25,000 lawyers' fees. We keep a lawyer employed. He don't do much else."[14]

The trade press also highlighted the industry's concerns about high-speed news distribution and the constant threat of libel, framing current law as outdated and insufficiently protective of the technically modern American press.[15] According to the *Fourth Estate,* "The honest news-presenting papers are in continual danger because they are all liable to mistakes."[16] Given the fast-paced work of the modern newspaper, *Newspaperdom* commented, "when the chances of [errors] being made is counted, it is really remarkable, not that there are a few in the hundreds of thousands of letters and words . . . but that there are so few."[17] According to the trade publications, libel doctrine of the 1880s and 1890s was "medieval," "outdated," and "anachronistic" and therefore "grossly unjust" because it failed to account for the modern institutional structure and practices of the newspaper industry.[18] The standards held journalists and their newspapers "guilty until proven innocent," the *Fourth Estate* claimed.[19]

Journalists' complaints reflected broader conceptual problems emerging in law. The complexity and interdependence of life in late nineteenth-century urban industrial America led to a fundamental rethinking of the very concept of causation in legal consciousness. All sorts of events that occurred in modern society came to be seen not as simple interactions or transactions, but as "the final links in long chains of causation that stretched off into a murky distance."[20] The problems were especially evident in the development of legal thinking and doctrine in tort law, which is the realm of law dealing with private wrongs—including libel—that cause a person harm or loss. Jurists debated where causal chains should be broken and who should be considered responsible for accidents, seeking "to bring order to the increasingly messy world that lay outside the courtroom" through ornate legal standards of liability.[21] The traditional standard was strict liability, which required no inquiry into motive or care in finding fault in the actions of a defendant. But legal thinkers worried that strict liability was an insufficient means of protecting the rights of individuals and entrepreneurs who acted carefully and with goodwill in conducting day-to-day business in an increasingly accident-prone world. Instead, they began to organize doctrine around the concept of negligence, which required an inquiry into the amount of care that a defendant should have demonstrated in the particular circumstances to avoid causing harm.[22] Critics also argued that because the strict liability approach lacked a moral inquiry into the cause of an act or the intentions of an actor, it wrongly allowed state intervention into the realm of private life through an unjust redistribution of wealth: either taking money from people attempting to engage in socially desirable economic activity and giving it to passive accident victims, or arbitrarily shifting blame and damages among equally faultless parties without a proper analysis of blameworthiness.[23]

In nineteenth-century cases involving speech, strict liability followed the model of the "bad tendency" test, a sweeping standard through which courts determined whether expression should be sanctioned based on its tendency to harm the public welfare. The test stemmed from the common law theory of English jurist Sir William Blackstone, who argued that although the law should prohibit government censorship of speech before it is spoken or published, post-publication sanctions were allowable for harmful speech.[24] Such harms could include undermining government authority, inciting violence, threatening public order, and offending standards of morality or public decency.[25] State and federal constitutional protections for freedom of speech and the press were generally not a primary consideration in these cases because, through the logic of the bad tendency test, they did not involve a prior restraint and because the focus was on the harmful outcome of the speech, not the intent of the speaker or publisher.

American courts categorically considered libel—false statements that were harmful to one's reputation—to have a bad tendency, and considered libel doctrine to serve the aim of maintaining public order by curbing press "licentiousness" and encouraging self-censorship among publishers who might otherwise wantonly attack the characters of public and private people.[26] The majority of courts ruled that the law did not protect false statements from sanction through criminal prosecution or civil suit; if such speech was privileged or protected it was because it was true and published without malice, not because of some greater benefit to society served by its publication.[27] In practice, both the criminal law of libel, which dealt with government prosecutions for alleged libels (often statements targeting government and its officials), and the civil law of libel, which typically dealt with lawsuits over statements about private individuals, operated through a "truth-plus" standard first articulated in 1804 by Alexander Hamilton in his defense of a printer in a politically charged criminal libel case. Hamilton had argued that the publisher should at least have the opportunity to show the jury the truth of the statement published, plus proof of his "good motives and justifiable ends" in publishing it.[28] The New York Supreme Court endorsed the "truth-plus" standard in an opinion by Judge James Kent, and the New York legislature formally adopted it as law in 1805. It gradually gained acceptance in most jurisdictions.[29] Thus, even if a newspaper defendant targeted by a civil libel suit was able to prove the truth of a statement at issue, the plaintiff was still owed damages for the harm incurred unless the defendant could also show the publication was not motivated by malice and was justified. Such was the balance struck in favor of protecting people from the harm of unwanted attention from the press.

The thinking of two of the era's most influential judges and legal theorists, Thomas Cooley and Oliver Wendell Holmes Jr., illustrates the special problems libel law raised as tort liability faced new conceptual challenges and complaints from the press. Cooley, the author of leading treatises on constitutional law and torts, and a member of the Michigan Supreme Court from 1864 to 1885, argued that motive and morality had no place in considerations of liability. In order to protect individual autonomy from government interference—a central purpose of law—legal analysis should focus exclusively on acts: "That which it is right and lawful for one man to do cannot furnish the foundation for an action in favor of another." Because analysis in civil cases must be based on external, objective standards, Cooley argued, liability should require no inquiry into "the good or bad motives which influenced the action. . . . Any transaction which would be lawful and proper if the parties were friends, cannot be made the foundation of an action merely because they happened to be enemies."[30]

Cooley viewed the press as a modern instrument of mass education and enlightenment in need of strong protection from government interference, and argued that leading cases in libel law placed too high a value on protecting the reputations of political and public figures while neglecting "freedom of discussion in public affairs."[31] The First Amendment required a broad conditional privilege in libel law for the discussion of matters of public concern, Cooley argued, whereby plaintiffs would bear the burden of showing that defendants acted maliciously and intended to cause harm. A privilege for fair comment on or criticism of politicians or their official acts had gradually and unevenly expanded throughout the nineteenth century,[32] and Cooley argued that the privilege should protect not just political speech but the vital social role of newspapers in modern society, as they sought to meet readers' expectations for "a complete summary of the events transpiring in the world, public or private, so far as those readers can reasonably be supposed to take an interest in them." Such a task would be impossible to accomplish, Cooley noted, "without matters being mentioned derogatory to individuals." A strong conditional privilege would ensure constitutional guarantees protecting freedom of the press, Cooley argued, and reflected the broader legal consciousness in a modern information marketplace where mistakes—especially those passed along the telegraph wire—were bound to occur. "Whatever view the law may take, the public sentiment does not brand the publisher of a newspaper as libeller [*sic*], conspirator, or villain, because the telegraph despatches [*sic*] transmitted to him from all parts of the world, without any knowledge on his part concerning them, are published in his paper, in reliance on the prudence, care, and honesty of those who have charge of the lines of communication, and whose interest it is to be vigilant and truthful."[33]

As a justice on the Michigan Supreme Court, Cooley encountered challenges in putting his abstract ideals about press freedom into practice, however, and his opinions reflected shifting views and growing uneasiness with the sensationalism of the late nineteenth-century press. In the 1882 case *Miner v. Detroit Post & Tribune Co.,* Cooley wrote the majority opinion ruling that a trial court should have extended a qualified privilege to the *Post* for a story that claimed a police judge was corrupt. The trial court erred, Cooley wrote, because it "put the case upon precisely the same footing with publications which involve merely private gossip and scandal, [as if] there is no difference in moral quality between the publication of mere personal abuse and the discussion of matters of grave public concern."[34] Just a year later, however, Cooley backed away from the privilege in a case that involved a story in the *Detroit Evening News* alleging a University of Michigan doctor had taken advantage of a female patient. In an order denying the publisher's request for a rehearing,

Cooley explained that the newspaper's claim of privilege was undercut by the jury's responses to special questions on the matter of damages. The jury had concluded that the "the publication was made in entire disregard of the plaintiff's rights" with the purpose of "sensation and increase of circulation." Cooley explained that although a conditional privilege should support the press in its important public service role, an absence of regard for an individual's rights, sensationalism, and greed were all sufficient proof of malice for a plaintiff to overcome the privilege. "A false and injurious publication made in a public journal for sensation and increase of circulation is unquestionably in a legal sense malicious," Cooley concluded.[35]

Cooley also narrowed the scope of his rationale for the conditional libel privilege in the 1883 edition of his treatise *Constitutional Limitations,* articulating boundaries around the subject matter the privilege should protect and reflecting a shifting idea about how he conceived of an acceptable journalistic report. In previous editions Cooley had rooted the privilege in the special social role the press served in modern democratic society, but the revised 1883 rationale extended no special status to journalists. Cooley wrote that a newspaper publisher should benefit from a privilege that covers information in the public interest "not because he makes the furnishing of news his business, but because the discussion is the common right and liberty of every citizen."[36] Moreover, Cooley's new rationale reflected a more nuanced and cautious view of the proper role of the newspaper in the public sphere: "It is one thing to reproduce in the newspaper injurious reports respecting individuals, however willing the public may be to hear them, and a very different thing to discuss the public conduct of a high official." Cooley's revised public-private distinction, based on the social role of the plaintiff, suggested an analytical consideration that would play a complicated role in the serial libel cases. Cooley argued that "a private individual only challenges public criticism when his conduct becomes or threatens to be injurious to others; public characters and public institutions invite it at all times."[37]

U.S. Supreme Court Justice Oliver Wendell Holmes Jr.'s contributions to the evolution of American legal thought are widely documented.[38] Like Cooley, his late nineteenth-century thinking on torts and libel law faced practical and conceptual challenges presented by modern life. Holmes's treatise *The Common Law,* first published in 1881, was a powerful articulation of the proper place of objective standards in private law. Holmes echoed Cooley's assertion that tort liability should be concerned with acts rather than motives: law deals with "external phenomena" and is "wholly indifferent to the internal phenomena of conscience," Holmes wrote. However, the subsequent removal of any questions of fault led toward strict liability, Holmes argued, leading to the problem of redistribution of wealth by courts, which was anathema to a system of justice built on preserving individual rights and limiting state interference with them. Rather than ask whether a defendant acted with malice or ill will, Holmes argued, questions of fault and blame should be considered from the perspective of whether actions aligned with accepted social customs, "ancient rules" unconsciously adopted over time. These customs were the objective standards required to make tort law consistent and predictable.[39]

However, Holmes's 1894 law review article "Privilege, Malice, Intent" acknowledged that the interplay of these three legal concepts threw into question the notion that tort law could be insulated from public policy considerations by judges reasoning from external, objective principles. Contrary to his argument in *The Common Law,* Holmes argued in "Privilege, Malice, Intent" that "phenomena of conscience"—including malice—could be essential to considerations of liability. Moreover, Holmes argued that the very idea of objective judicial decision making in a realm of law insulated from public policy had become theoretically problematic.[40] The problems were starkly evident in the consideration of late nineteenth-century libel cases, where standards for what constituted defamatory statements could be subjective and there were clear public policy reasons to hold the press legally accountable in otherwise personal disputes.

Two of Holmes's judicial opinions—in the 1891 case *Burt v. Advertiser* and the 1909 case *Peck v. Tribune Co.*—illustrate an interpretation that differed significantly both from Cooley's approach to privilege and Holmes's evolving thinking on tort liability more broadly. *Burt v. Advertiser,* a case before the Massachusetts Supreme Judicial Court, involved a series of stories, some of which had been based on the reports of other newspapers, about an individual's alleged involvement in a corruption scandal in the New York customs office. The *Advertiser* urged the court to recognize a conditional privilege for discussion of matters of public concern that was reflective of Justice Cooley's early thinking: because the article involved a subject of public importance, it should be privileged. Holmes rejected the

*Advertiser*'s position. Although the article indeed involved a topic of public interest, Holmes explained, "the so called privilege of fair criticism upon matters of public interest" did not extend to "facts [that] are not true."[41] More importantly for the doctrine related to serial libel cases, Holmes also rejected the *Advertiser*'s assertion that its reliance on other newspapers for the story "tended to prove that the [newspaper] had reasonable cause to believe the charges to be true." Belief in the truth of the story did not constitute a defense, Holmes concluded, invoking a succinct and often-used statement of the rule with regard to a publisher's supposed intentions or lack of malice: "A person publishes libellous [*sic*] matter at his peril."[42] Holmes's view of acceptable forms and practices of journalism, according to *Burt v. Advertiser,* simply did not offer an allowance for passing along false information without first verifying it.

*Peck v. Tribune Co.,* which Holmes wrote for the majority on the U.S. Supreme Court, reiterated the limited defenses available to newspapers when they claimed a libel was the result of a mistake. The *Chicago Tribune* faced a libel suit over a photo accompanying an advertisement for Duffy's Pure Malt Whiskey. The photo, which purported to show a nurse who recommended Duffy's "as the very best tonic and stimulant for all weak and rundown conditions," was actually a photo of Elizabeth Peck, who was not a nurse and who was, in fact, a "total abstainer from whiskey and all spirituous liquors."[43] The Seventh Circuit U.S. Court of Appeals in Chicago ruled that Peck could not sustain a claim for libel because the false statements did not amount to defamation per se, that is, they did not, on their face, harm her reputation.[44] Justice Holmes and the U.S. Supreme Court reversed the lower court, ruling that Peck's case should go before a jury. Although there may be "no general consensus of opinion that to drink whiskey is wrong or that to be a nurse is discreditable . . . an unprivileged falsehood need not entail universal hatred to constitute a cause of action," Holmes wrote. The *Tribune*'s claim that the advertisement was published by mistake offered no defense, Holmes argued, in a matter-of-fact statement: "'Whatever a man publishes he publishes at his peril.' The reason is plain. A libel is harmful on its face. If a man sees fit to publish manifestly hurtful statements concerning an individual, without other justification than exists for an advertisement or a piece of news, the usual principles of tort will make him liable, if the statements are false or are true only of some one else."[45]

In *Peck,* Holmes provided a blunt articulation of the basic outlines of the civil libel doctrine that newspaper defendants confronted in the 1890s and early 1900s. The standard reflected a narrow view of the idea of a report that gave little leeway when false facts were printed about private people, accidentally or otherwise. While much of tort law in the preceding decade had shifted toward a consideration of negligence in liability—asking whether parties acted with reasonable care and with good motives—libel law did not follow this shift. Libel cases involving large news publishing operations could prompt the same types of problems that convoluted causal chains and muddied liability across the fast-industrializing corporate world, but judges were generally disinterested in publishers' motives or intent, at least as a question of liability, when cases involved false statements about individuals or affairs not related to politics.[46] Faultlessness rarely arose in libel cases, because a culpable publisher could usually be identified, and although the publisher might have claimed that the libel was the result of a mistake, he or she could not claim that it was a blameless accident for which no one could be held responsible in a legal sense. Indeed, the doctrine even extended to the role wire services played in distributing news, as courts held that organizations like the Associated Press, as well as the newspapers that used those services, could be considered independently liable, as well as jointly liable, for the publication of defamatory news.[47] Even a conditional privilege for such mistakes had failed to catch on widely and had been curtailed by Cooley, its key proponent. So instead of seeking to limit their liability, news publishers sought to limit the damages they owed to plaintiffs.

When a news report was defamatory and neither true nor privileged, the plaintiff was entitled to an award of damages. As attorney Henry Sackett explained in an 1899 pamphlet on libel law for *New York Tribune* reporters and editors, "How small the sum [of damages] shall be will depend on how good a case the defendants can make out in mitigation of damages."[48] Awarding damages required attaching a dollar amount to a loss that was difficult to measure and which the plaintiff was not required to prove having lost. Moreover, libel could trigger punitive or exemplary damages, described by legal treatise authors as intended "to signify [the jury's] sense of a defendant's conduct by fining him to a certain extent . . . in excess of the amount which would be adequate compensation for the injury inflicted on the plaintiff's reputation," and to "impose a punishment on the defendant, and hold him up as an example to the community."[49] Legal treatises explained that juries had wide latitude to award punitive or exemplary damages when they thought the situation warranted doing so. Evidence could include "all the circumstances attending the publication," including a showing that the defendant was "culpably reckless or grossly negligent in the matter."[50] Juries were also sometimes instructed to consider a plaintiff's "distress of mind" or "hurt feelings" when weighing punitive or exemplary damages.[51] Plaintiffs did not have to show actual injury to recover punitive or exemplary damages for libel, but juries could not award more than they claimed to have lost, so "plaintiffs generally [took] care to make their claim of damages sufficiently large."[52] This helps explain the shockingly large amounts some plaintiffs demanded.

Journalists joined with critical voices in the judiciary in claiming that punitive and exemplary damage awards in libel cases wrongly played a public policy role in private law and left important matters of rights and responsibilities to what Holmes called the "more or less accidental feelings of a jury."[53] Samuel Merrill, editor of the *Boston Globe,* attorney, and author of the 1888 book *Newspaper Libel: A Handbook for the Press,* argued, "The whole principle upon which punitive damages are based seems to be inherently wrong." The proper legal venue for punishing an act was criminal law, not civil law, Merrill argued, and to offer juries the opportunity to assess punitive damages "is to constitute every man a prosecuting officer." Merrill contended that in libel cases, "the power to award a verdict which shall at the same time compensate the plaintiff and punish the defendant, proves too often a ready means of gratifying spite on the part of a prejudiced jury."[54] The problem of punitive damages was reflected in the legal consciousness surrounding libel law such that it drove many of the retraction statutes that journalists' trade organizations pushed in the 1890s and early 1900s.

Appealing an award of damages because it was excessive or insufficient was a difficult task. Whether juries awarded huge punitive damages, or tiny nominal amounts, judicial standards were not clear about the limits of damage awards in either direction. According to treatise author John Townsend, "A case must be very gross, and the damages enormous, to justify ordering a new trial on a question of damages." On the other hand, Townsend explained, "there is nothing to forbid the granting a new trial, in a proper case, for insufficient damages," but this was "of rare occurrence."[55] Moreover, the amount a jury awarded and the evidence it took into account in calculating the award was subject to the instructions of the judge presiding over the trial, so an appeal over damages often had to claim a legal error was made in those instructions. The law was slightly clearer on the ability of appeals courts to question trial court instructions, but not in a way that helped publishers that challenged them. In 1878, the U.S. Supreme Court ruled that such instructions were "entitled to a reasonable interpretation," and it directed that "appellate courts are not inclined to grant a new trial on account of an ambiguity in the charge to the jury."[56]

Newspapers in cases involving accidental defamation could not challenge the fact of their liability, and appeals over excessive awards were rarely successful, but they could present evidence to try and mitigate the amount of punitive or exemplary damages awarded to the plaintiff. As Sackett explained in his 1899 pamphlet, "The principle underlying all the . . . defences [*sic*] is that they tend to show an absence of actual malice."[57] "Actual malice" did not have the same legal meaning in nineteenth-century libel law that it has today. Also called "express malice," it was defined as "ill will or wicked intent." A jury could award plaintiffs punitive or exemplary damages beyond the general damages the plaintiff suffered when the plaintiff could provide evidence of actual malice. On the other hand, a publisher could present evidence tending to disprove actual malice and limit the damages awarded to the plaintiff to only general damages.[58] In 1964's *New York Times v. Sullivan* and a series of cases that followed, the U.S. Supreme Court would give the term actual malice a different and more specific meaning in libel cases involving public officials and public figures: knowledge of the falsity of a defamatory statement before its publication, or "reckless disregard" for whether it was true or false.[59] The nineteenth-century conception of "ill will or wicked intent" was broader and more open to judicial interpretation than today's standard, and the type of evidence that parties were allowed to present to either prove or disprove actual malice could vary from case to case, state to state, and across federal jurisdictions, helping to contribute to a sense among publishers—and emphasized by the trade press—that the law was unfair due to its unevenness and unpredictability.

Theodore Sedgwick, author of the 1891 *Treatise on the Measure of Damages,* wrote that the rule for mitigation of exemplary damages included "all circumstances which negative the existence of malice, or show the malice to have been little." Such circumstances included "good faith, the advice of counsel, or belief of right." However, if the defendant showed an absence of actual malice, but acted in a "cruel and abusive manner," exemplary damages could still be awarded. "Thus," Sedgwick wrote, "though the defendant honestly believed the slander he published to be true, yet he published in a wanton and reckless manner, or maliciously, the plaintiff may recover exemplary damages."[60] Courts varied in their determination of what types of circumstances could demonstrate "good faith" or a lack of actual malice in cases arising out of mistakes in the industrialized late nineteenth-century press. In particular, as bad news traveled fast along wire services around the country, an important and common question was whether a publisher could mitigate damages by showing that a defamatory statement was republished, without malice, from another source.

One leading case on the question of republication, cited and quoted extensively in libel law treatises and case law, was *Dole v. Lyon,* an 1813 case in which Judge James Kent wrote for New York's highest state court that the publisher of the *Troy* (New York) *Northern Budget* could not defend himself from a libel suit by claiming that he had simply republished a defamatory letter written by a third party.[61] To recognize such a defense, Kent argued, "would be no check on a libelous printer, who can spread the calumny with ease and with rapidity throughout the community," adding that "the injury is inflicted by the press, which, like other powerful engines, is mighty for mischief as well as for good." The publisher's proposition that the court consider republication as a defense was "as destitute of foundation in law as it is repugnant to principles of public policy," Kent argued, which required that "individual character must be protected, or social happiness and domestic peace are destroyed." It was important that a civil cause of action be available to individuals in instances of republication not just to discourage libel, but also to ensure that those who suffered reputational harm had some means to sue and collect damages, Kent contended. "It is not sufficient that the printer, by naming the author, gives the party grieved an action against him," Kent explained. "The author may be some vagrant individual who may easily elude process; and if found, he may be without property to remunerate in damages."[62]

In the late 1800s, however, a few courts suggested that some circumstances surrounding republication could offer proof of lack of malice, making room in the idea of a report for forgivable accidents. In 1876, the Minnesota Supreme Court ruled in *Hewitt v. Pioneer Press* that the *St. Paul Pioneer Press* could mitigate damages by presenting evidence showing that other local newspapers had published similar stories to the one at issue, leading the *Pioneer Press* publisher to believe his article was true when he published it.[63] An 1887 case in the federal district court for Western Missouri offered a different and more expansive rationale for protecting republication, rooted in the social role of newspapers in democratic society. In *Edwards v. Kansas City Times,* future U.S. Supreme Court Justice David Brewer explained to a jury that the *Times*'s claim that it republished a defamatory article it found "in a responsible sheet" should be part of the jury's consideration of damages "because it is a function and duty of newspapers to furnish information to its readers of the current events." Brewer's rationale echoed Cooley's conception of a doctrine that reflected the reality of the modern news marketplace and the expectations of readers, going so far as extending a "right" to the public to receive information: "It would be a physical impossibility to send an agent to every place, where events, tragedies are transpiring, to ascertain by personal examination the exact facts. A paper could not give us all which we have a right to hear of the current events of the day." Although the jury should "see to it that plaintiff is compensated for the injury which her character has sustained," in the form of general damages, Brewer concluded, "while doing that you are not required to render such a verdict as will put a check and stop upon the legitimate pursuit of information in respect to matters of public interest."[64]

Overall, however, the balance of juridical opinion at the turn of the twentieth century was that cases like those involving the *Pioneer Press* and *Kansas City Times* were exceptions to a broad republication rule.[65] As the Michigan Supreme Court put it in *Atkinson v. Detroit Free Press,* an 1881 case in which Justice Cooley made a strident dissenting call for a qualified privilege, "no doctrine is better settled."[66] Republishing a libelous story might be a genuine mistake, but libel doctrine did not offer it much chance as proof against malice. Rather than embrace a concept of press freedom that tolerated errors by the industrialized press in the interest of their value to society, as a few jurists proposed, most courts tended to hold to traditional standards enshrined in doctrines, treatises, and the legal consciousness surrounding libel: "Tale-bearers are as bad as tale-makers" and "whatever a man publishes he publishes at his peril."[67]

In spite of arguments from journalists and prominent judges about the need to protect newspapers, mistakes and all, for their value to an informed democratic society, American courts at the turn of the twentieth century were mostly unwilling to recognize new rules that would supersede the traditional strict liability standard and place the rights of newspapers to publish the news over the rights of individuals to maintain a good reputation. Libel doctrine sharply illustrated the conceptual difficulty in maintaining separate private and public legal spheres in tort law, as one of the doctrine's central aims was to maintain "social happiness and domestic peace" by encouraging respectful discourse in the public sphere, especially by those "who can spread the calumny with ease and with rapidity throughout the community."[68] This mix of private and public ends provided a key rationale for treating libel differently from other realms of tort law, where negligence standards developed as a response to industrialized complexity in modern business. The motive and intent of a publisher and the care with which editors and reporters gathered and published news only mattered for purposes of lowering the financial impact of a ruling against them and could only limit their liability when the publication was true or protected political criticism. The trend toward sensationalism and speed in journalism helped convince many judges that their role in libel law was less to draw clear distinctions between public and private law, and more to mind the boundary between permissible speech and that which tended to disrupt public order by harming individuals. The proper purpose of libel law, according to this position, was to encourage caution and restraint in the press by applying strict liability standards that protected individuals' reputations from the perils of an industrialized institutional press.

The tension that this legal doctrine created at the meeting point of freedom of the press, commercial competitiveness, and the interest in preventing and compensating reputational harm was on full display in the serial libel cases that played out between Juliette Smith, Edward Rutherford, Tyndale Palmer, J. F. de Freitas, Annie Oakley, and the newspapers that defamed them between 1890 and 1907. The press's response to the challenge that the cases and doctrine presented—urging judges and legislators across the country to acknowledge a broader idea of a journalistic report by striking a balance that protected their fallible use of wire services as part of a booming business model and a vital social role in the democratic public sphere—was a key moment in the development of legal consciousness surrounding press freedom in America.

CHAPTER 3

# *THE SMITH AND RUTHERFORD CASES*

–·–·/·–/···/·/···/

## THE NEWS AS "A WRONG AND PERILOUS SYSTEM"?

On June 8, 1890, Juliette C. Smith boarded a train in Toronto, Canada, bound for New York City to meet her husband, a wealthy and well-known Toronto merchant named John C. Smith. Joining her on the journey was Edward Rutherford, a friend of the Smiths and a man with whom, according to witnesses in Mrs. Smith's libel suits, she "was known to be on terms of intimate acquaintance."[1] John Smith later testified that he knew his wife and Rutherford would be on the train together—in fact the two men had planned the trip—and he met them both at Grand Central Station when they arrived in New York.[2] However, some of the newspapers that received wire service news from the United Press Association painted a different picture of the intentions of Mrs. Smith and Mr. Rutherford: according to the story filed by a Toronto-based correspondent, they had absconded from Toronto with plans to elope in New York, and Mr. Smith, after receiving a telegram about their plan, had hurried there to confront them. The *New York Evening Sun* gave it the headline "Did She Go with a Handsomer Man? Reported Sensational Elopement in Canadian High Life."[3] Rutherford and Smith were identified in the story by only their last names, but courts that heard the subsequent libel suits ruled that any person acquainted with them could identify them from the article.[4]

The serial libel suits of Rutherford and Smith were a result of sensationalism, inaccuracy, and industrialized speed. Their litigation reflected changing ideas about tort liability and the role of the press in the public sphere. In defending themselves, newspapers formulated a wire service defense and libel syndicate defense. The wire service defense centered on a claim that the burden of damages should be diminished in light of the accidental nature of the libel. Newspaper defendants argued that their important social role in speedily disseminating news required that they trust wire services for the accuracy of their reports, and that the publication of bad news in these instances should not be considered sufficiently malicious to justify an award of punitive damages. The theory of the libel syndicate defense was that jurors could conclude a plaintiff had already been sufficiently compensated for the overall harm done by a libel, and award a smaller amount of damages to a particular defendant, if they knew about the plaintiff's other cases and their outcomes.[5] The two new defenses reflected newspaper defendants' response to conflict in the social negotiation of the idea of a report, as they sought to protect the vital role the telegraph and wire services played in their businesses. They led judges to reflect on what constituted fair compensation when a newspaper defendant claimed to have committed an unavoidable error in completing its public duty. The appellate courts' rulings and their rationales reflected both doctrinal and philosophical differences about what constituted an acceptable journalistic report.

The basis for Smith's and Rutherford's lawsuits was that the false claim (that they were involved in an illicit affair) harmed their reputations. In the early 1890s, an "imputation of a want of chastity to a female, married or unmarried," was libelous per se, meaning the plaintiff did not need to plead or demonstrate additional contextual facts to prove that she was defamed. As Newell explained in the 1890 edition of his treatise on libel and slander, adultery, fornication, and prostitution were illegal in almost every state; therefore, accusing a woman of being unchaste—even in language that was not explicit—was equivalent to accusing her of committing a crime.[6] The Court of Appeals of New York, the state's highest court, called adultery "the gravest offense that can be committed by a wife and mother."[7] In suits that played out between 1890 and 1897, juries awarded Smith $7,500 in her suit against the *New York Sun,* $4,000 in her suit against the *Buffalo Morning Express* and *Illustrated Express,* and $15,000 in her suit against the *Chicago Herald.* Rutherford won his suit against the *New York Morning Journal,* although the damage award was not specified in the appellate record.[8]

As the newspapers appealed the trial court rulings, the fact that the libelous story came from a wire service played a central role in their arguments, connecting the commercial imperative of using the telegraph to gather and publish interesting news to the legal imperative of minimizing newspapers' exposure to litigation. The publishers contended that they should have been allowed to mitigate the damages the jury was able to award by raising a wire service defense at trial: the fact that they considered the United Press and its Toronto agent to be trustworthy sources of information, and published the story in their usual "course of business," should have been considered proof of a lack of actual malice and should therefore have precluded or limited the punitive or exemplary damages available to Smith or Rutherford.[9] The wire service defense that the newspapers sought to present pivoted on the contention that it would be impossible to expect newspaper publishers or editors to fact-check every single item they published, and, at any rate, an absence of caution in that regard did not necessarily prove a presence of actual malice for the purposes of awarding punitive or exemplary damages. For example, the *Morning Journal,* in its appeal to the Second Circuit U.S. Court of Appeals in New York, argued that "it would be a physical impossibility for a newspaper to send an agent to every place where events are transpiring to ascertain by personal examination the exact facts, and that, if such a rule were insisted upon, 'a paper could not give us all which we have a right to hear of the current events of the day.'"[10] In the Chicago case, the *Herald* argued that "it had been misinformed by an agent selected with due care and caution," and that the story was "selected with reasonable care."[11]

In two of the cases, the newspapers claimed that trial court judges' jury instructions harmed their cases by indicating that their failure to verify the story could justify awarding punitive damages. In *Smith v. Sun Printing & Publishing Association,* the trial judge had allowed the paper to present evidence explaining that its report had come from a wire service, but the *Sun* claimed the judge unfairly undermined the paper's defense in his explanation to the jury of punitive damages. "If you think that the fact that the article was received, in the ordinary course of business, from a reliable . . . news agency, is sufficient to excuse the defendant from the duty of investigation, of inquiry, of delay, for the sake of accuracy, before it published this most damaging article, then you will not give punitive damages" the judge said. "If you think that the defendant was guilty of reprehensible negligence in publishing the article without further attempts to verify its truth, then you are justified in giving such a reasonable sum in damages as shall be an example to deter against similar future negligence."[12] Similarly, in *Smith v. Matthews,* the publisher of the *Buffalo Morning Express* and *Illustrated Express* argued that the trial judge erred in telling the jury, "You may find actual malice if you find [the newspaper] failed to make an investigation as to the truthfulness of the charge."[13]

The fact that the defamatory story came from a wire service also played a role in the *New York Sun*'s libel syndicate argument: that the number and outcome of Smith's other lawsuits for the same libelous story should factor into the jury's calculation of damages. The trial judge had refused to allow the *Sun* to present testimony related to any of Smith's other libel suits. Judge Emile Henry Lacombe of the Second Circuit U.S. Court of Appeals dismissed the *Sun*'s argument that the defense should have been available. Any evidence about other lawsuits arising out of the same United Press story "was wholly irrelevant and immaterial," Lacombe ruled. "That other newspapers, which published similar libels, had been prosecuted by the plaintiff for their acts, was a matter with which neither court nor jury had any concern."[14]

Moreover, in *Morning Journal v. Rutherford, Smith v. Sun,* and *Smith v. Matthews,* state and federal appeals courts in New York ruled that the wire service defense lacked a basis in legal doctrine or principle, and ruled that it was unpersuasive and unreasonable. The federal district court in *Smith v. Sun,* for example, noted that "in actions for libel the amount of damages is very peculiarly a matter for the jury," and that the *Sun* had failed to show the "gross error, prejudice, perverseness . . . corruption" or "undue motives" necessary to overturn its verdict.[15] The courts cited libel cases in which juries awarded punitive damages not only where there was evidence of "bad faith" or "malice," but also where there was "recklessness," "carelessness," or "wantonness."[16]

The appellate judges' rejection of the wire service defense mixed doctrinal interpretation with criticism of the newspapers' careless use of news wires in gathering and publishing news where individual reputation and the existing doctrine of libel were concerned. Judges were reluctant to second-guess jurors' conceptions of why the newspapers' practices failed to meet the legal or social standard for an acceptable journalistic report, and in some instances explicitly agreed with them. According to federal district judge Nathaniel Shipman, it was reasonable to conclude that jury members were not prejudiced or hostile toward the *New York Sun* in awarding Smith $7,500, but rather that they found the newspapers' use of the wire in gathering and publishing news without first verifying it to be "a wrong and perilous system."[17] Judge Theodore Bartlett of the New York Court of Appeals, the state's highest court, wrote in *Smith v. Matthews* that although he did not conclude that the *Buffalo Morning Express* and *Illustrated Express* were "impelled by a wicked intent to injure this plaintiff," he also observed that "it was not their custom, on receiving articles of news, to ascertain their truth or falsity before publication. The publishers who adopt this reckless rule in the conduct of their business must abide the consequences."[18] According to Bartlett, the consequences for such a reckless approach to gathering and publishing a journalistic report properly included punitive or exemplary damages.

More than any other judge who heard appeals in the Smith and Rutherford cases, however, Judge Lacombe combined concerns about the careless practices of the press with outrage at the flawed news values the stories demonstrated. In his July 1892 opinion in *Morning Journal v. Rutherford,* Lacombe wrote "there was no excusable motive" for the newspaper's publication of "a bit of spicy gossip dealing with the domestic infelicities of private persons . . . and to publish it without making any effort to verify its truth was a piece of reprehensible negligence which may be fairly characterized as wanton."[19] In another opinion, denying the *New York Sun*'s motion for a new trial in April 1893, Lacombe rejected the *Sun*'s argument that the trial judge prejudiced the jury when he made negative statements about the newspaper from the bench. "That the comments in this particular case were harsh is manifestly due to the circumstance that the facts in the case were what they were," Lacombe wrote. "When, in his discretion, [the judge] decided to express an opinion as to the libel, it is not easy to perceive how he could have said much less."[20]

Lacombe was outraged not just because the newspapers had carelessly published a falsehood about Smith and Rutherford, but because they defended this gross invasion of privacy as part of their role in serving the public interest. "That the public has such a right to be informed as to the private life of every individual, as to the domestic affairs of every family, as to the happiness or infelicity which may characterize every household, as will warrant the proprietors of newspapers who cater to its wants in publishing any falsehood they may think interesting to their readers, without any investigation as to its truth, is a proposition . . . to which this court is not prepared to assent," Lacombe wrote.[21] He was not the only judge troubled by the unwanted publicity cast upon Smith. Judge Bartlett wrote that an award of less than $4,000 might have "answered the purposes of justice" in Smith's case against the Buffalo newspapers; however, the jury's decision was acceptable given that "this publication was grossly negligent, and attacked, without the shadow of justification, the good name of an innocent wife and mother, charging her, in effect, with unfaithfulness to her marriage vows, and the abandonment of her children."[22] Lacombe and Bartlett not only saw no value in a standard that could limit the punitive damages levied against careless and sensational newspapers, they also saw harm in denying those damages to private individuals who did not seek the publicity cast upon them by bad news. Their opinions reflected the dominant legal consciousness that libel was meant to protect innocent individuals from the harms of carelessly published bad news as well as a broader conception that acceptable journalism should exclude such reports, regardless of whether they were true or false.

Not all appellate judges shared the views of Lacombe and Bartlett, however, and two other opinions suggested alternative theories of liability in libel in cases involving wire services and serial libel, one of which favored the press's version of what should be considered acceptable forms and practices in a journalistic report. In the first of three appeals in *Smith v. Matthews*, an intermediate New York state appeals court rejected the *Buffalo Morning Express* and *Illustrated Express*'s assertion of a wire service defense. Instead, however, the court applied a strict liability theory known as *respondeat superior*, or the master-servant doctrine. Under this doctrine, an employer shares liability for the acts of an employee or agent.[23] Applying this rule, the court found that the newspaper could not shift blame or liability to the wire service or an individual reporter or editor. "When the defendants had provided means of publication and intrusted [*sic*] to an agent the discretionary power of publishing or rejecting, investigating or taking chances of the truthfulness of an article," the court ruled, "his recklessness becomes theirs, and it rested with the jury to characterize the act and withhold or award punishment."[24]

Meanwhile, Judge Edward F. Dunne of the Circuit Court of Cook County, Illinois, applied an analytical approach that stood in stark contrast to the judicial opinions of the New York judges.[25] Dunne granted the *Chicago Herald*'s motion to set aside a jury's $15,000 damage award to Juliette Smith in May 1894.[26] Dunne's ruling relied on a theory of liability that placed some of the responsibility of the harm with the plaintiff rather than the defendant, couched in a criticism of her actions surrounding the libel claim and a discussion of the modern public service role of the press.

Dunne asserted that Rutherford and Smith must have known, along with "all intelligent persons . . . that news is gathered by such a paper [as the *Herald*] from multitudinous sources, and from the whole face of the earth, and published hot from the telegraph wires." Further, they must have known "that it is absolutely impossible for this modern engine of information to do the work which the times and the people expect and demand, and at the same time verify every item and explore for possible falsity in what seems true." Indeed, just like the New York papers, the *Herald* did not argue the story was true or its publication justified; it maintained that it had been misinformed, and that no one associated with the newspaper knew Smith or had "malice of any sort toward her."[27] Dunne further observed that "neither the plaintiff, nor her husband, nor anyone on her behalf" notified the *Herald* about the offending article or requested a retraction or apology; the editors said they found out about the error when the lawsuit was filed more than two months after the article was published. Smith also "made no effort . . . to punish, either civilly, criminally, or otherwise, the correspondent who was the author of the article." In other words, Dunne wrote, "the party claiming to be injured by the circulation of a falsehood did not a thing to stop its further circulation, or to diminish the evil resulting from the publication."[28] Dunne drew an analogy to cases involving physical injuries and breach of contract that reflected a standard of assumption of risk which acknowledged when the harmed party was partially at fault.[29] In both types of civil cases, Dunne said, the injured party was "required by law" to take reasonable steps to lessen the injury in order to succeed on a later civil claim.[30] Moreover, Smith provided no proof of "any monetary damage, or any actual loss of social standing" as a result of the story published in the *Herald,* although she was also entitled to compensatory damages for her mental and physical suffering, Dunne wrote, "and to punitive damages in the discretion of the jury."[31]

With regard to the $15,000 damage award, Dunne concluded that although "it is exceedingly difficult to draw the line at a certain figure and say what is just and unjust," his independent examination of libel cases in Illinois and other states in which verdicts were reversed for excessive damages convinced him that "to allow this verdict to stand . . . would be not only in defiance of all precedents, but a plain violation of justice."[32] Newspaper publishers "must answer for wrong done even without express malice, but they are entitled to fair treatment," Dunne wrote.[33]

Although the $15,000 damage award qualified as excessive according to Dunne's comparison to other libel cases, his decision to overturn it was unusual in comparison to the other Smith and Rutherford cases. The courts that refused to overturn a jury's award to Smith or Rutherford as excessive argued that to do so required evidence that the jury was actuated by "improper motives" such as passion or prejudice against the defendant.[34] Although this was an inexact standard and one that tended to prevent reversals, it was more in line with common law standards.[35] Dunne did not propose that there were improper motives or prejudicial coercion at the trial level in *Smith v. Chicago Herald.* Rather, he found that the jury's award was not in line with other awards for libel, without specifically naming an amount that would have been appropriate.

Although libel law was a frequent topic in the trade press of the early 1890s, neither the Smith and Rutherford cases nor the emerging serial libel issue in general made big waves. Standing in isolation and playing out over five years amid dozens of other libel cases, some of which involved more salacious facts or prominent plaintiffs, it could be that the Smith and Rutherford cases were not considered worthy of coverage or did not appear to be the beginning of a worrisome trend. Also, the trade papers tended to depend on editors and reporters to send them items related to libel law and other issues, and the lack of coverage may have also been due to disinterest or unawareness among those reader-contributors. *Newspaperdom* offered a tepid editorial position on the wire service defense, making note of the Smith and Rutherford cases but not taking a firm or reflective stance, and offering instead strategic advice and a caution for editors and publishers in their use of wire service news. In July 1894, the trade paper advised editors to take care in publishing wire service reports that they had not independently verified. The article quoted a *Philadelphia Ledger* editorial that argued, "Making the newspaper, and all those who contribute to it, responsible for [their] statements . . . best honors journalism by maintaining [its] integrity." It also reprinted part of a *Lorain* (Ohio) *Herald* editorial that rejected the contention that "an editor is no more responsible for what he prints than is the telegraph operator for the message he sends over the wire." Instead, the editor "is morally and legally responsible for what he prints, whether he writes it or not," *Newspaperdom* counseled readers, adding "certain other dailies . . . might not have had . . . the judgments for libel against them secured by a Toronto lady, if they had in fine working order such a rule and had applied it to the verification of wired reports, whether from special correspondents or news associations."[36] The editorial stands in stark contrast with the legal arguments of the newspapers targeted by Smith and Rutherford. While those publishers argued their liability should be limited by a wire service or libel syndicate defense, *Newspaperdom* viewed an acceptable journalistic report as one that was the result of thorough verification, no matter the source, with the legal responsibility falling to a paper that failed to verify.

Standard professional practices contradicted the advice *Newspaperdom* provided and its version of the idea of a report, however. The serial libel cases bear out the fact that selecting and publishing wire service news without checking its truthfulness was altogether common in the competitive newsrooms of the late nineteenth century. In the courts, newspaper defendants in the Smith and Rutherford cases formulated specific legal defenses meant to protect their practices in publishing telegraphic news. Wire services had become a vital part of the news business, and the publishers' legal arguments reflected a concern that libel doctrine could limit or even eliminate their ability to collect and publish interesting news—and to maintain their financial viability—if doing so required burdensome verification practices or raised a constant threat of large libel verdicts. Newspaper defendants did not argue they should be able to abrogate their responsibility for printing libel altogether, but rather that the law should limit the potentially devastating effects of accidents that they considered to be almost inevitable.

The appeals court decisions represented two opposing views on the newspapers' defenses and the rationale supporting them, reflecting competing conceptions of the role of the telegraph and wire service news in journalism and standards of liability. In the New York cases, judges considered the newspapers' printing of the story about Smith and Rutherford to fall well within the standards of "carelessness" or "wantonness" required to justify awards of punitive damages, regardless of their having come from a wire service. At the same time, the courts concluded that if the juries that awarded punitive damages did so out of their offense and outrage at the newspapers' practices, that motivation did not amount to the "improper motives" that would necessitate a reversal for excessive damages. The courts accepted the verdicts and rejected the wire service or libel syndicate defenses the newspapers proposed to mitigate damages. It was reasonable and not prejudicial, the courts reasoned, for juries to consider the newspapers' practices "wrong," that is, invasive of privacy or likely to harm reputation, and "perilous," that is, careless or wanton, even if the libel could be explained as accidental. These decisions reflected the logic of bad tendency and strict liability: any publisher of a libelous statement is responsible for the resulting harm to an individual's reputation and the damages assessed were a matter solely left to the discretion of the trial judge and jury, absent a serious legal error or clear evidence of prejudice. The decisions endorsed an idea of a report that emphasized accuracy and verification over speed and sensationalism.

Meanwhile, Judge Dunne struck a wholly different balance in overturning the damages awarded to Smith in her case against the *Chicago Herald*. Under Dunne's analysis, Smith and Rutherford had a responsibility, like victims of other types of accidents, to take basic steps to minimize the harm caused by the false story, and they did not do so. The *Herald* was certainly at fault for whatever harm it caused by publishing the false story about Smith and Rutherford, but the liability was not the *Herald*'s alone—the plaintiffs also had a duty to attempt to minimize the harm caused by the accident, Dunne argued. His reasoning accepted the logic of the wire service defense, and his criticism of the plaintiffs' motives in filing the suits suggests he would have entertained the libel syndicate defense had it been presented. Moreover, his opinion was more accepting of an idea of a report that made room for the risk created by speed and acknowledged the public desire for fast news on a wide range of topics. The newspapers' use of wire services to meet that desire required legal leeway for the possibility that mistakes—including accidental libel—might occur.

The difference between the appeals courts' framing of legal responsibility in the Smith and Rutherford cases also reflected a difference in drawing lines among rights to reputation, information, and free expression that was at the core of the serial libel cases and the press's campaign for a legislative solution. The key source of outrage in Lacombe's opinions—and a pivotal difference in his and Dunne's interpretations of the serial libel cases—was the press's broader contention that the story about Smith and Rutherford fit into a framework of acceptable journalistic reporting that should be legally protected because it enriched a public right to information through their free expression. Lacombe said he was not willing to assent to the idea that any public or press right extended into "the private life of every individual, as to the domestic affairs of every family, as to the happiness or infelicity which may characterize every household."[37] The individual right to reputation was more important than the public's interest in the purported affairs of socialites or the press's aim to satisfy that interest, Lacombe argued. Dunne, on the other hand, concluded that although newspapers had a duty to take care where the reputational rights of individuals were concerned and "answer for wrong done," newspapers had a right to "do the work which the times and the people expect and demand" and to employ the technology of the day in so doing.[38] As the Smith and Rutherford cases came to a close in the mid-1890s, a new and more large-scale set of serial libel suits was already underway, prompting the coinage of the label "libel syndicate" along with a new urgency to solve the commercial and legal problem that the label was meant to describe.

CHAPTER 4

# *THE PALMER CASES*

–·–·/·–/···/·/···/

## THE FIRST LARGE-SCALE LIBEL SYNDICATE

In early October 1892, newspapers across the country reported a brazen theft in the emerging electric light business. According to the story that appeared in hundreds of newspapers via the United Press Association wire service, Tyndale Palmer, an employee of the Auer Incandescent Light Company, had been sent to Brazil to negotiate the sale of patent rights for a new light bulb. The story reported that in Rio de Janeiro, Palmer sold the patent for $510,000, but told Auer it was sold for only $70,000, splitting the remaining $440,000 with a local hotel owner named Joao Francisco de Freitas.[1] The shocking tale of international business fraud turned out to be a fabrication, and Palmer and de Freitas proceeded to gain notoriety from newspaper publishers not as swindlers, but as libel plaintiffs. Over the next ten years, Palmer (and in five cases, de Freitas) pursued lawsuits against hundreds of newspapers for printing the false allegations. The trade publication the *Fourth Estate* called it "the greatest libel syndicate of the age," a term both accurate and ironic.[2] On one hand, the term conveyed an apt description of Palmer's systematic approach to the litigation and a fair accusation that he was driven more by profit motive than a desire to repair his reputation. On the other hand, the *Fourth Estate* may have overlooked the fact that "libel syndicate" could also be a criticism leveled at professional practices that resulted in the efficient mass dissemination of defamatory bad news via news wire services.

The story about Palmer and de Freitas raised a similar legal scenario to the story about Smith and Rutherford. However, the Palmer cases played out very differently, reflecting a more complicated relationship between the social conception of an acceptable journalistic report and the legal consciousness surrounding standards of libel law. Juries rarely awarded large damages to Palmer, and appeals court opinions generally contained more cold legal reasoning than heated rhetoric, two outcomes that showed less outrage at the content of the faulty news story and less sympathy for the plaintiff Palmer. The scale of Palmer's legal campaign was truly reflective of the vast influence of the wire service network, and encouraged more publishers to assert a libel syndicate defense, but judges were not any more willing to accept it than they were in the Smith and Rutherford cases. The appellate courts based their decisions on a growing body of law that addressed the specific subject of serial libel and the libel syndicate and wire service defenses, while elaborating less on the broader legal theories of rights and responsibilities at play in the cases.

Another contrast to the Smith and Rutherford cases was how the boundaries of an acceptable journalistic report were debated and articulated. While appellate judges' opinions played the most visible role in drawing lines around what should or should not be fodder for news reports in the earlier cases, it was trial court juries in the Palmer cases that took a more significant role in drawing those lines. The nominal amounts awarded to Palmer in many of his suits suggest that the story about his alleged financial embezzlement was more in keeping with public expectations about what was appropriate news for the public sphere. In other words, the story was bad news insofar as it was false and harmful to the plaintiff's reputation, and therefore should trigger legal liability for newspapers that published it. However, by awarding minimal damages, jurors signaled that they did not otherwise consider the story to be offensive or excessive by intruding on the plaintiff's personal affairs.

Palmer was a businessman, and he employed an entrepreneurial approach in his litigation. He learned that the story was first reported in the October

1, 1892, *Philadelphia Times,* sent by telegraph to the main United Press office in New York City, and then sent on to wire service subscribers. Palmer identified the newspapers that published the story, and sent letters to them demanding that they retract it and compensate him for the harm done to his reputation. When the newspapers refused or—more often—printed a retraction but declined to send him money, he sued them. Palmer's attorney, John S. Dove of Philadelphia, contacted lawyers in cities and towns where newspapers had published the story and asked them to serve as counsel on the lawsuits, for a contingent fee.[3] In other cases, Palmer acted as his own attorney.[4] Palmer did not follow through with all the lawsuits he threatened or filed, and courts dismissed them when he failed to appear in court or did not pay a bond, a payment needed to secure a trial. Newspaper and trade press coverage of the lawsuits described a system whereby Palmer would decide whether or not to pursue suits in a particular state depending upon the outcome of his first case—what the papers referred to as a "test case."[5]

Palmer was also strategic in filing his suits. For example, he targeted newspapers in Mansfield, Youngstown, Canton, and Cleveland, Ohio, all of which were near Kilgore, Ohio, where he was born.[6] Palmer went to college and worked for a time in Washington, Iowa,[7] and he sued several newspapers in eastern Iowa, as well as the state capital, Des Moines. He lived and worked in Minneapolis and Philadelphia,[8] and he sued newspapers in Minnesota and Pennsylvania. But Palmer also sued newspapers in places where a direct connection is not so obvious: in New York City, where any businessman of the late 1800s would presumably want to maintain a reputation for honesty, but also in cities and towns in upstate New York like Buffalo, Rochester, Syracuse, Utica, Cortland, Lockport, and Rome. He filed several suits in Massachusetts, and at least one each in Maine, Wisconsin, Illinois, and Georgia. He sued two newspapers in St. Louis and four in Indianapolis.[9] Palmer's strategy appears to have been based on several factors. He was more likely to be able to show reputational harm in places where he had lived and worked such as Ohio, Iowa, and Minnesota. He also was more likely to succeed in jurisdictions such as New York, which had already established an opposition to serial libel defenses in the Smith and Rutherford cases. In one instance, Palmer successfully had a case removed from Illinois to New York because the defendant newspapers had sufficient subscribership there.[10] But his "test case" approach also demonstrated a willingness to sue anywhere that the allegedly libelous wire service story was published, even without a clear personal connection or jurisdictional rationale.

Palmer's damage claims were usually between $20,000 and $100,000 per lawsuit. De Freitas's usually matched Palmer's claims in his five suits.[11] Although an exact count of Palmer lawsuits may be impossible to establish through documentary evidence, it is clear that the crusade was immense and far-reaching. The *Winona* (Minnesota) *Republican* reported the number was 126 as of fall 1894.[12] At the May 1897 trial in Palmer's suit against the *Buffalo Illustrated Express,* an attorney for the newspaper claimed that the number was "152, or thereabouts," but Palmer's attorney objected and Palmer refused to confirm that number.[13] At the high end, the *Fourth Estate* speculated in its November 24, 1898, edition that "when he has concluded his litigations he will have sued 600 daily newspapers."[14] One reason a specific number is so difficult to determine is because Palmer sometimes dropped or abandoned the suits, while he settled others out of court. Even those that reached a judge or jury are difficult to document since they were filed all over the country at a time when the quality and consistency of judicial record keeping varied from courthouse to courthouse.

Few juries awarded Palmer significant damages, and none awarded the full amounts to which he claimed to be entitled. Palmer's largest award was $7,500 in his suit against the *New York Daily News.*[15] A jury in Youngstown, Ohio, awarded Palmer $1,350 in his suit against the *Telegram* in November 1896.[16] Of the forty-seven suits listed in a table accompanying the *Fourth Estate*'s July 22, 1897, report about Palmer's cases, twelve were listed as having been decided in the plaintiffs' favor. The twelve included the *New York News* verdict for Palmer, as well as a $50 award against the *Rome Sentinel;* six cents against the *Rochester Post Express;* six cents against the *Buffalo Illustrated Express;* $150 against the *Syracuse Herald;* $25 against the *Utica Observer* (which dropped to $10 on a retrial after Palmer's appeal); $50 against the *Cortland Standard;* $58.75 against the *Hornellsville* (New York) *Tribune;* $1.50 against the *Canton* (Ohio) *Repository;* and 6 and one-quarter cents against the *Pittsburgh Leader.* De Freitas reportedly won $10 in his suit against the *Utica Observer,* and six cents against the *Rome Sentinel.* Twenty-one of the cases identified by the *Fourth Estate* were listed as dismissed, most because Palmer had failed to pay a bond. One was "not tried yet," another was "never tried," and a third labeled "no trial." Two cases—one against the *Courier* of Waterloo, Iowa, and the other against the *Republican* of Cedar Rapids, Iowa—were listed as having been won by the defendant newspaper.[17]

Some newspapers settled with Palmer or de Freitas out of court, and most of the settlements were considerably larger than the plaintiffs' typical trial award. According to the *Fourth Estate,* as of July 1897 the *Boston Herald* and *Cleveland World* had each settled with Palmer for $500, the Brooklyn *Eagle* for $1,500, the *St. Louis Republic* for $1,000, and the *Pittsburgh Dispatch* for $1,200. The *St. Louis Post-Dispatch* settled with each plaintiff for undisclosed amounts.[18] There is little information in the historical record explaining exactly why the publishers that chose to pay Palmer a settlement did so, but it is likely that they believed that a court case would be more costly and complicated than a settlement—another illustration of how the press's legal decisions had as much to do with commerce and self-preservation as they did with principle. The *Fourth Estate* argued that uncertainty about state libel laws tended to push newspapers toward settling.[19]

In another contrast to the Smith and Rutherford cases, in the Palmer cases newspapers and the trade press engaged the court of public opinion as well as the court of law, a realm in which they had unmatched potential for influence. Much of the discourse extended the press's case for why their reporting practices should be considered socially acceptable into the legal consciousness surrounding libel, incorporating commercial rationales into legal ones. Newspapers reporting the lawsuits—often including their own involvement in them—mixed straightforward reportage with editorial explanations and excuses for their publication of the allegedly defamatory article. The trade press's strategic role was also more pronounced, advising newspapers targeted by Palmer, de Freitas, or other libel plaintiffs that—contrary to the choice some publishers were making—they were better off to fight the cases in court than to settle them.

Some newspapers sued by Palmer appealed to their readers by framing their professional practices as an acceptable, if not failure-proof, means of gathering a report to inform the public.[20] For example, the *Winona* (Minnesota) *Republican* explained that it had mistakenly published the false accusations about Palmer and de Freitas because the "dispatch was received in the usual course of business from a news agency . . . upon which [the *Republican*] relied for accuracy." When informed of the error, the paper "cheerfully and in terms unequivocal made full and complete retraction of said charges." Having stated its defense, the paper explained to its readership of possible jurors its rationale for fighting the case:

> Mr. Francisco De Freitas being at the time of this publication a resident of South America and Mr. Palmer engaged in business in London, in neither of which places *The Republican* circulated, it felt that neither of these men had suffered through the publication either in their property, trade, occupation, or good name, and believed, such being the case, that the retraction would be accepted. But retraction and vindication are not what these men were seeking.[21]

Other newspapers shifted the blame for errors onto the wire services. The *Youngstown* (Ohio) *News* observed, "All are liable to make mistakes. The United and Associated Press make them nearly every day of the year. . . . The newspapers using the service of these two news gathering associations make a big mistake in calling the attention of the public to the blunders made by these creditable institutions."[22] It is likely that the *News* wanted to avoid suits like its local competitors the *Vindicator* and *Telegram* had faced, and its publishers believed that the more the local newspapers reported incidents like the one involving Palmer, the more likely serial libel suits would become. Of course, it was risky to point a finger at how problematic news wire services could be while simultaneously considering them essential to the news business.

A few days after a jury in Jackson, Michigan, awarded Palmer $100 (he had sued for $25,000), the *Jackson Citizen Patriot* sought to burnish its reputation and reiterate its legal defense. "The Citizen printed the dispatch in good faith, as a matter of news, coming through a channel it regarded and had always found reliable," the paper explained. Readers should be more troubled by the waste of public resources than by the harmless mistake, it continued: "Palmer secures $100; the people of Jackson County pay over $184 in additional court expenses created by the suit. And the Citizen, which had no malice against Palmer or anybody else, and did no intentional or actual wrong, is required to pay $100." The newspaper further sought to dissuade future libel plaintiffs, observing that, after Palmer paid his lawyer's fees, the remainder of his damage award "will scarcely cover his railroad and boarding house expenses here."[23]

Covering libel cases could place the press in an awkward position regarding the idea of a report that it sought to promote. Priming an audience of potential jurors about the altruistic intentions behind mistakenly printing libel before a trial or asserting a lack of negligence after the trial could help a newspaper's cause. However, the benefits of giving greater attention to libel cases and their plaintiffs were debated among the press. Negative coverage of an ongoing trial could carry the threat of contempt of court,[24] and members of the journalistic community worried that covering the cases might encourage more plaintiffs to file them—a strategy in direct conflict with the journalistic value of informing the public.[25] Again, though, newspapers had to consider these principles alongside the economic realities of the serial libel threat, to their bottom line as well as their business model.

Trade publications, meanwhile, gave muted support to the idea of coverage embargoes on libel suits as a means to slow the creeping tide of libel litigation,[26] and reminded publishers that, in light of such cases "the vigilance of the copy editor should be in no degree relaxed."[27] They expended more ink encouraging newspapers to fight, rather than settle, the cases they faced. The rationale presented by the *Fourth Estate* was twofold, and both parts had implications for social consciousness surrounding the idea of a report. In the particular cases of Palmer and de Freitas, juries were likely to award damage amounts smaller than the average settlement because of their lack of familiarity with the plaintiffs and a perception that the alleged libel at the center of the suit was not a harmful or offensive one. In other words, even if they lost, newspapers were not likely to face the crippling damage awards Palmer demanded. The trade paper cited, among other cases, the paltry $10 verdict Palmer won against the *Utica Observer* as evidence that courts and juries were sympathetic to newspapers. It called the $7,500 verdict against the *New York Daily News* an exception, "with every prospect of a reversal." Publishers could expect friendly treatment from juries, even if the law and the facts were not on their sides, because Palmer and de Freitas "might just as well have lived with the man in the moon so far as the public was interested in them . . . and the damage done them was theoretical and problematic," the *Fourth Estate* explained.[28] In other words, a false report that otherwise fit the public's expectations of acceptable forms and practices of journalism could work in a newspaper's favor in a libel suit. Although the prediction about the verdict against the *New York Daily News* was wrong—it was upheld on appeal[29]—the logic underlying the trade paper's editorial advice that most juries would be more sympathetic to the local newspaper than to these unknown businessmen appears to have some support. Awards like the one levied against the *New York Daily News* were unusual—much smaller awards were more typical in Palmer's cases—and he chose not to follow through on other cases when the newspapers refused to settle them. Newspapers that settled cases indeed paid more than what juries typically awarded, according to the *Fourth Estate*'s research.[30]

Moreover, the Palmer cases represented a larger concern about the growth of similar types of legal campaigns, and discourse about them reflected the connection between commercial and legal imperatives for the industry. For example, the *Fourth Estate* warned, "Publishers should bear in mind that every one who consents to a compromise [i.e., settlement] makes it harder for the others" by encouraging Palmer to continue the crusade.[31] Some journalists believed that the best way to discourage other potential Palmer-like plaintiffs was to demonstrate that "the bringing of libel suits against newspapers is not likely to be found a sure avenue to riches." The trade paper's research into the cases helped its editors conclude that the Palmer suits "prove[d] . . . that mulcting of newspapers innocent of wrong intention is not easy."[32]

It is difficult to know for certain why the juries that handed Palmer or de Freitas small or nominal damage awards did so, but the contrast with the Juliette Smith and Edward Rutherford cases is worthy of attention. Jurors hearing the Palmer cases might have considered a false accusation of embezzlement not as offensive as those who heard the cases involving false accusations of Smith and Rutherford's elopement. Citizens in Buffalo for example, might have been no more familiar with a socialite from Toronto than a light bulb salesman from Philadelphia, and jurors in either case would have heard testimony involving a similar lack of editorial care regarding wire service news. The fact that one Buffalo jury awarded Smith $4,000 in her case against the *Illustrated Express* in 1893 and another awarded Palmer a nominal six cents in his case against the same paper in 1897 suggests that the Palmer report fit a social conception of acceptable news because it was considered less intrusive or offensive than the one involving Smith, or that it was a more forgivable mistake.[33]

Moreover, the distinctly different interpretations provided by two appellate judges provide some insight into jurors' thinking about what constituted an acceptable form of reporting, and how it could differ by location. Palmer's largest award, the $7,500 granted by a New York jury against the *New York Daily News,* was affirmed by Judge William Rumsey of New York City's intermediate appellate court and later the state's highest court. Rumsey rejected the *News*'s claim that the award was excessive. He contended that the false allegation to the *News*'s 100,000 readers that Palmer had stolen thousands of dollars was a serious blow to a man who relied on the "the confidence of those who employed him."[34] It is reasonable to conclude that the New York jury that awarded Palmer $7,500 thought similarly. In Pennsylvania, on the other hand, the state supreme court rejected Palmer's appeal of an award of six and a quarter cents, reasoning that it was just as likely that his few business or social connections in Pittsburgh led jurors to have difficulty in finding specific harm done by the false story.[35]

Indeed, it was usually Palmer, and not the newspaper publishers, who sought relief from the appellate courts.[36] The premise of Palmer's appeals was similar to that of the newspapers involved in the previous round of serial libel cases: he argued that erroneous jury instructions had led to an inappropriate damage amount. But Palmer argued the damage amount was smaller than was fair, not larger. In appealing trial court decisions against the *Pittsburgh Leader* and the *Buffalo Illustrated Express,* for example, Palmer argued that the juries' awards of nominal damages—six and one-quarter cents and six cents, respectively—should be overturned.[37] Palmer also appealed three successive trial court decisions in his case against the *Utica Observer,* arguing in each appeal that the trial court improperly allowed the *Observer* to present evidence in its defense.[38] As with the Smith and Rutherford cases, appellate courts refused to overturn jury verdicts without evidence of juror prejudice or corruption. The Pennsylvania Supreme Court, for example, explained that a Pittsburgh jury's award of nominal damages to Palmer was "not necessarily absurd."[39] The court found that the trial judge had properly explained that any amount of damages, from nominal up through punitive, could be awarded. The jury's decision reflected nothing more than the conclusion that he had not suffered actual damages, considering "where the newspaper circulated and the absence of evidence that [Palmer] resided or had business or social relations therein."[40]

Several of the newspaper defendants in New York sought to cast doubt on Palmer's legal motives in the form of a libel syndicate defense, arguing that they should be able to present evidence about the number and success of Palmer's other lawsuits as a means of mitigating their own liability for damages. For example, the *New York Daily News* argued that the trial judge should have allowed the newspaper to introduce evidence showing that Palmer had sued numerous other newspapers for publishing the same article, and that his total claim of damages exceeded $200,000.[41] On the other hand, Palmer's appeal of his six-cent verdict against the *Buffalo Illustrated Express* was based in part on the contention that the trial court should not have allowed lawyers for the newspaper to question him on the witness stand about five letters he sent to the newspaper, one of which made the following reference to his numerous libel suits: "The financial loss to me from the publication as a whole was most serious. However, I do not expect any one paper to bear it all, but only its due proportion."[42]

The *Daily News* also sought to raise a wire service defense in order to limit its liability for damages. The paper's publisher testified in a pretrial hearing that "he did not consider it necessary in general to verify such items as he received from the United Press," because the *News* "had employed the United Press . . . for a considerable length of time, and that it placed confidence in the accuracy of the information which it received" from the wire service.[43] In an interesting twist, the trial judge allowed the newspaper to proceed with the wire service defense, but also allowed Palmer to introduce evidence that could undermine the contention that United Press was in fact reliable. Palmer called to the stand "the attorney in the action of Smith against this defendant (N.Y. News Publishing Co.), and proved by him that he brought an action against this defendant for libel on the 13th of June, 1890." Given the timing, the witness was in all likelihood an attorney for Juliette Smith in a libel suit against the *News,* and Palmer's intention was to show that the *News* had in fact recently been in a very similar situation for relying on false news relayed by the United Press, resulting in a libel case.[44]

Judge Rumsey and New York City's intermediate appellate court knocked down the *Daily News*'s attempts to assert both a libel syndicate defense and a wire service defense in June 1898, in a ruling that was affirmed by the state's highest court seven months later. In a lengthy opinion citing Juliette Smith's suit against the *New York Sun* and an 1897 libel suit against *New York Herald* publisher James Gordon Bennett, Rumsey echoed Oliver Wendell Holmes: "The true rule is and must be, that whoever publishes a libel, publishes it at his peril, and he cannot mitigate his damages because some other reckless or evil-disposed person has incurred the same liability that he has for the same story."[45] Addressing the libel syndicate defense, Rumsey explained, "When several persons unite in the publication of one libel, a tort is committed by each one of them for which he severally is liable to the plaintiff, and the plaintiff is entitled to a judgment against each one for all the damages which he suffers."[46] Addressing the *News*'s contention that the jury should be allowed to consider the fact that the offending item was sent by a normally trustworthy wire service, Rumsey simply stated, "The fact that it was published in reliance upon the statement of some other person is not a defense."[47] The court ruled that the evidence that the *News* and Palmer presented concerning United Press's reliability, including the testimony offered by Smith's lawyer about an earlier suit against the *News,* was immaterial to the case.

New York's highest court offered a slightly different rationale in rejecting the *Buffalo Illustrated Express*'s assertion of the wire service and libel syndicate defenses. A lower appeals court ruled in favor of the newspaper in May 1898, denying Palmer's motion for a new trial and ruling that by taking the stand in his own defense and agreeing to discuss letters that he and the newspaper sent to each other after the story was published, Palmer assumed a risk that information that was detrimental to his case could be raised in court.[48] However, the Court of Appeals of New York reversed the lower court's decision in February 1900, focusing its analysis not on Palmer's decision to take the stand and testify about the letters, but on the content of the letters, which included information about other newspapers that had published the damaging story and the other suits that Palmer had filed.[49] Judge Celora E. Martin, writing on behalf of the unanimous seven-member court, said that "it is now too well settled to be questioned that the fact that others have published the same libel which was unknown to the defendant when the publication complained of was made, or that suits have been commenced against others for the publication of such libel, is inadmissible. The defendants in this case were liable, and that some one else was also liable was immaterial." Martin cited Judge Rumsey's opinion in the *New York Daily News* decision, the Second Circuit's 1893 ruling in Juliette Smith's case against the *New York Sun,* and several others in New York, Illinois, California, and the Seventh Federal Circuit.[50]

Thus, Palmer won most of his cases in the sense that the newspapers were considered liable for harming his reputation, and appellate courts did not forgive errors based on use of the wire services or allow evidence that exposed Palmer as a serial plaintiff. However, juries did not award Palmer the large amounts he demanded, or nearly what Smith or Rutherford recovered in their suits. The frequent awards of nominal damages indicated that the trade papers were right: juries were not offended by the content of the false article about Palmer in the same way that they were by the article about Smith and Rutherford. As the appellate courts generally reinforced an inflexible libel doctrine, the jury awards in the Palmer cases demonstrated that the doctrine did not necessarily pose an existential threat to every newspaper targeted in a serial libel suit, particularly where jurors could see a report as libelous but otherwise aligned with their news values.

Moreover, the cases showed that a gap existed between what jurors considered far enough outside the realm of an acceptable journalistic report to assess heavy damages, and the legal consciousness reflected in appellate judges' willingness to accept a wire service or libel syndicate defense. While courts ruled that reporting false information should lead to legal consequences via strict liability, the burden of damages could be lessened when the report fit the profile of information distributed via wire service that served the public interest without being salacious or intrusive.

Palmer's serial cases demonstrated the profound potential for an entrepreneurial plaintiff to use libel law to create nationwide headaches for an industrialized, sensationalistic, turn-of-the-century press that was heavily dependent on the telegraph to distribute news. Although newspapers made little progress in their courtroom appeals for a wire service and libel syndicate defense, juries may have embraced the logic underlying the press's arguments about how the report at issue reflected their broader social role. The cases also began to generate serious discussion of the serial libel issue among editors and publishers, who considered ways to protect their business interests without depending on the courts moving away from strict liability standards. In the meantime, however, collecting and publishing bad news from the wires remained a potentially expensive peril, especially if a case came along involving a more sympathetic plaintiff or a more outrageous story.

## **TABLE 1:** The *Fourth Estate*'s List of Palmer and De Freitas Suits

The list is edited for formatting, style, and clarity but otherwise is as it appeared in "Those Tyndale Palmer Libel Suits," *Fourth Estate*, July 22, 1897. According to the article that accompanied the list, the information regarding the suits was submitted to the trade paper by newspaper editors and publishers.

| | AMOUNT (IN DOLLARS) SUED FOR | AMOUNT (IN DOLLARS) OF COMPROMISE | VERDICT (IN DOLLARS) FOR | REMARKS |
|---|---|---|---|---|
| Rome (New York) *Sentinel*<br>(Palmer)<br>(De Freitas) | <br>15,000<br>10,000 | | <br>50.00<br>.06 | |
| Mansfield (Ohio) *Shield* | 50,000 | | | Case dismissed |
| Keokuk (Iowa) *Constitution* | 50,000 | | | Case dismissed, did not furnish bond |
| St. Paul *Dispatch* | 50,000 | 350.00 | | |
| Indianapolis *Journal* | 50,000 | | | Dismissed; no bond |
| Indianapolis *News* | 50,000 | | | Dismissed; no bond |
| Indianapolis *Sun* | 50,000 | | | Dismissed; no bond |
| Indianapolis Amer. *Tribune* | 50,000 | | | Dismissed; no bond |
| Pittsburg *Dispatch* | 100,000 | 1,200.00 | | |
| Youngstown (Ohio) *Vindicator* | 50,000 | | | Dismissed |
| Rochester *Post-Express* | 20,000 | | .06 | |
| St. Louis *Post-Dispatch*<br>(Palmer)<br>(De Freitas) | <br>50,000<br>50,000 | | | Settled out of court; amount not stated |
| St. Louis *Republic* | 100,000 | 1,000.00 | | |
| Springfield (Massachusetts) *Union* | 10,000 | | | Default; no bond |
| Syracuse *Herald* | 20,000 | | 150.00 | |
| Utica *Observer*<br>(Palmer)<br>(De Freitas)<br>Cases appealed and verdict reduced to $10. | <br>25,000<br>25,000 | | <br><br>10.00 | First verdict $25; dismissed; "No cause for action" |
| New York Daily *News* | 25,000 | | 7,500.00 | Case appealed. |
| Milford (Massachusetts) *Journal* (Palmer)<br>(De Freitas) | <br>10,000<br>10,000 | | | Dismissed; did not furnish bond |

| | AMOUNT (IN DOLLARS) SUED FOR | AMOUNT (IN DOLLARS) OF COMPROMISE | VERDICT (IN DOLLARS) FOR | REMARKS |
|---|---|---|---|---|
| Lockport (New York) *Journal* (Palmer) (De Freitas) | 10,000<br>10,000 | 50.00 | | Each paid own costs |
| St. Cloud (Minnesota) *Times* | 100,000 | | | Case dismissed |
| Savannah (Georgia) *Press* | 20,000 | | | Not tried yet |
| Portland (Maine) *Argus* | 20,000 | | | Dismissed; no bond |
| Appleton (Wisconsin) *Crescent* | 100,000 | | | Dismissed; no bond |
| St. Paul *Pioneer Press* (De Freitas) (Palmer) | 50,000<br>50,000 | | 50.00 | Dismissed; new trial asked and denied |
| Winona (Minnesota) *Republican* | 100,000 | | | Case dismissed |
| Waterloo (Iowa) *Courier* | 20,000 | | | Plaintiffs lost suit |
| Cedar Rapids (Iowa) *Republican* | 100,000 | | | Case lost |
| Oil City (Pennsylvania) *Blizzard* | 10,000 | | | No trial |
| Huntington (Indiana) *Democrat* | 100,000 | | | Dismissed; no bond |
| Duluth (Minnesota) *Evening Herald* | 30,000 | | | Never tried |
| Brooklyn *Eagle* | 25,000 | 1,500.00 | | |
| Boston *Herald* | 100,000 | 500.00 | | |
| Canton (Ohio) *Repository* | 50,000 | | 1.50 | |
| Cleveland *World* | 50,000 | 500.00 | | |
| Cortland *Standard* | 25,000 | | 50.00 | Each paid own costs |
| Des Moines (Iowa) *News* | 100,000 | | | Dismissed; no bond |
| Fort Dodge (Iowa) *Chronicle* | 50,000 | | 25.00 | Def't paid cost |
| Hornellsville (New York) *Tribune* | 10,000 | | 58.75 | |
| Lafayette (Indiana) *Journal* | 50,000 | | | Settled for costs |
| Pittsburg (Pennsylvania) *Leader* | 50,000 | | .06¼ | |
| | 2,100,000 | 5,100.00 | 7,895.43¼ | |

# CHAPTER 5

# *THE OAKLEY CASES*

–·–·/·–/···/·/···/

## LIBEL AND CELEBRITY

Annie Oakley, unlike Juliette Smith, Edward Rutherford, J. F. de Freitas, or Tyndale Palmer, was well known to the general public long before she made headlines as a serial libel plaintiff. Throughout the 1880s and 1890s, Oakley rose to fame across the United States and Europe as the spunky female star of Buffalo Bill's Wild West show, a popular traveling circus. By 1903, Oakley and her husband, Frank Butler, were living comfortably in New Jersey, Oakley having left the Wild West show and now contemplating an acting career.[1] On August 11 of that year, three Chicago papers—the *American, Examiner,* and *Tribune*—reported that Oakley had been arrested, charged, fined, and sentenced to jail the previous morning at the Harrison Street police court for stealing a man's pants in order to buy cocaine.[2] The irresistible story promptly spread via the Scripps-McRae and Publishers Press Association wire services, and soon papers across the country were reporting the "Fall of Annie Oakley."[3] Her friends clipped the story from newspapers across the country and sent them to her, and she reacted swiftly and angrily. On August 12, she wrote to the *Brooklyn Union Standard,* "Woman posing as Annie Oakley in Chicago is a fraud," adding that she had "not been to Chicago since last winter" and that rather than destitute she owned "property enough to live on." She wrote, "Now that you have done me an injustice in publishing that article, I hope you will contradict it." To the *Philadelphia Press* the next day she jotted, "Contradict at once. Someone will pay for this dreadful mistake."[4] She followed through on the threat with dozens of libel suits.

The Oakley suits demonstrated how the right combination of factors could amount to a serious, widespread legal threat arising from newspapers' reliance on wire service news. As in the Smith and Rutherford cases, and in contrast to the Palmer cases, jurors in the Oakley cases were likely to be offended at false reports that the plaintiff was a penniless, larcenous drug addict, which could offend their sense of an acceptable journalistic report and result in large damage awards. The fact that Oakley was famous and well regarded was likely to magnify the offensiveness and the amount awarded. Meanwhile, the Palmer cases had shown that courts' refusal to accept a wire service or libel syndicate defense could benefit a plaintiff who was determined to pursue a large-scale crusade. Thus, the Oakley cases presented a scenario that many editors and publishers had feared, and which the previous serial libel cases had made apparent: the careless use of wire service reports to feed and stoke public interest in salacious news allowed an item of bad news about a highly sympathetic, well-heeled plaintiff to create a sudden and serious financial burden for newspapers. They could argue that the harmful publication was an unfortunate but unavoidable function of social expectations for salacious news delivered at high speed, but without courts' acceptance of this economic imperative as part of the legal consciousness surrounding serial libel, the threat to newspapers could be severe.

Oakley filed fifty-five libel suits against newspapers across the country. The libel suits consumed much of her and her husband's time and energy for the next seven years, as she crisscrossed the country to appear in courtrooms from Massachusetts to Kansas, Michigan to Louisiana. Like previous serial libel plaintiffs, Oakley demanded damage amounts in the tens of thousands of dollars in her lawsuits. An extensive report on the Oakley cases compiled by Publishers Press Association attorney Louis Stotesbury and published by the *American Printer* in 1905 listed fifty of the suits, with the smallest claims being $5,000 against two papers in Dayton, Ohio, the *Journal* and *Herald,* as well as the Richmond (Virginia) *News Leader.* Oakley sued fourteen of the papers for $10,000, nineteen of them for $25,000, the

Scripps-McRae wire service for $30,000, Publishers Press for $50,000, and the *Toledo Times and News Bee* for $75,000.[5] She tended to win larger amounts than Palmer, figures closer to the amounts awarded to Smith and Rutherford. In another contrast to the Palmer cases, newspapers that settled with Oakley generally paid less than those that went to trial.

Although Oakley had been the subject of false press reports before, the story of the arrest was the first that spurred lawsuits. For example, while the Wild West show was touring Europe, false reports had surfaced that she was engaged to marry an English nobleman. And in December 1890 and January 1891, while she was spending Christmas in England with her husband, French newspapers reported that she had died. Oakley's obituary appeared in newspapers across the United States. Oakley and her husband appeared to take the incident mostly in stride, spending several days of their holiday sending hundreds of letters and telegrams to newspapers, friends, and family correcting the mistake. But Frank Butler confided to a friend that the episode "affected Annie terribly."[6]

Oakley owed much of her notoriety and success to frequent and favorable news coverage, and she knew it. In 1894 she told the *New York Press,* "I guess the press has made me famous. But you know, some really peculiar things have been said."[7] The false story about drug-induced larceny amid squalor in Chicago was more than "peculiar," however. The "terrible piece . . . nearly killed me," Oakley told the *Joliet* (Illinois) *Daily News* in 1906. "The only thing that kept me alive was the desire to purge my character."[8] Oakley's positive public image was vital to her livelihood, and the fact that she did not sue over earlier false reports of her marriage or death suggests that the story of destitution and cocaine addiction posed an especially serious threat to that image.

Oakley and Butler contended that, contrary to popular opinion, the numerous suits did not result in great wealth. In a 1910 letter to *Forest and Stream,* Frank Butler rebutted the idea. "I only wish it was true," Butler wrote, "but any one who has had any lawsuits knows that they cost money, and wherever it was possible to do so she had the best attorneys. They come high, but are the cheapest in the end."[9] But the amount that Oakley accrued in trials and settlements also suggests that the libel campaign was not a losing endeavor. In the first three years of litigation, according to journalistic and appellate records, Oakley collected over $42,000 in twenty-seven lawsuits.[10] The 1905 *American Printer* list included nine suits in which juries had levied verdicts against the newspapers, including $5,000 against the *New Orleans Times-Democrat,* $3,000 against the *Hoboken* (New Jersey) *Observer,* and $900 against the *Scranton* (Pennsylvania) *Truth.*[11] In addition, the October 27, 1906, issue of *Forest and Stream* reported that a jury had awarded Oakley $27,500 against "one of the yellow journals of Chicago." Although the magazine did not identify the newspaper, it was probably either the *American* or the *Examiner,* both of which had published the story and were owned by William Randolph Hearst, who was known for advocating a more sensationalistic approach to journalism.[12] Trial judges reduced some verdicts, finding that they were excessive. The $5,000 award against the *New Orleans Times-Democrat* was originally $7,500.[13] The *Fourth Estate* reported that a trial judge in Cincinnati lowered a verdict against the *Cincinnati Post* from $9,000 to $2,500.[14] In Rochester, New York, juries hearing cases against the *Times* and *Herald* could not agree on a verdict and were dismissed.[15] The *American Printer* report also listed several settlements, including three newspapers in Des Moines, the *News, Capital,* and *Register Leader,* all of which paid Oakley $750 apiece, and the *St. Louis Globe-Democrat,* which paid $1,250.

In the appellate courts, the wire service defense played a more complex role in the Oakley suits than in the earlier serial libel cases, but the results were mostly the same for newspapers. According to Stotesbury's report in the *American Printer,* the story about Oakley received skeptical criticism from some editors and reporters when it was first reported, who sought to follow up in due diligence. For example, *Chicago American* reporter George Pratt, who was among the first to report the story, was familiar with the Wild West show and some of the people connected to it, and had questioned the woman extensively in her jail cell about the show and her role in it, satisfying his skepticism about her identity. Moreover, a Scripps-McRae wire service manager in Cleveland, having read the story in the *Chicago Tribune* on the morning of August 11, instructed a Chicago-based reporter, Ernest Stout, to follow up on it before sending it out via the Scripps-McRae and Publishers Press Association wires. Stout verified the *Tribune* story with a police inspector before writing up his version and sending it out on the wire.[16] Thus, editors were not careless, and were arguably engaging in precisely the processes of verification that the trade press encouraged as a part of an acceptable journalistic report.

However, as appellate courts applied strict liability standards and a limited view of how newspaper defendants could mitigate their damages, such due diligence did not necessarily help them. In appeals involving the *Scranton Truth* and *Cincinnati Post,* the newspapers argued that trial judges erred in refusing to admit depositions related to the initial reporting of the stories in Chicago, evidence that could allow them to mitigate their damages by addressing whether the wire service report was reliable and whether their use of it was reasonable or reckless. In both cases, the courts ruled that testimony or evidence related to exactly what happened in Chicago that fateful morning would prolong and complicate the proceedings with irrelevant details. Judge Robert Archbald of the U.S. District Court of Pennsylvania ruled that "to allow [the *Scranton Truth*] to . . . lay before the jury all that was said and done—relevant and irrelevant—in and about the Chicago police court, which gave rise to the article, of which neither the defendants nor the readers of their paper had the slightest knowledge, would be to obscure the issue." Moreover, Archbald pointed out, "in the present instance . . . there was the added circumstance that the original journal had published an intermediate retraction."[17] In other words, the *Truth* could not defend itself by saying that it relied on the accuracy of the *Philadelphia Press* story it had copied when, before the *Truth* even printed its version, the *Press* had retracted the original. Archbald relied heavily on Judge Emile Lacombe's earlier rebuttal of the *New York Morning Journal* and its "reckless indifference to the rights of others" in a case involving Edward Rutherford.[18] Meanwhile, in the case involving the *Cincinnati Post,* the 6th Circuit U.S. Court of Appeals simply ruled that although the facts might show how the Scripps-McRae Press Association gathered and sent the story to subscribing papers, those facts were irrelevant because they "were not known to the defendant prior to the publication, and therefore could in no degree have affected its action."[19] These courts were uninterested, as a legal matter, in determining how the interplay among professional standards and practices, technology, and human error contributed to the accident that harmed Oakley's reputation.

The narrow view of what constituted relevant facts also limited newspapers' opportunities to use a libel syndicate defense in the Oakley cases. For example, in an order granting a motion for a new trial between Oakley and the *Hoboken Observer,* the New Jersey Supreme Court ruled that the trial judge "properly overruled testimony to show the particulars of actions brought against other newspapers for publishing a similar libel and the amount of damages received in some of those suits."[20]

On the other hand, in Oakley's appeal of a six-cent verdict in her suit against the *Elmira* (New York) *Daily Gazette and Free Press*, Judge Alden Chester of the intermediate New York appeals court considered the press's practices to fit his view of an acceptable journalistic report. Oakley argued that the trial judge should not have admitted evidence related to the initial reporting of the stories in Chicago and their transmittal through the wire services to the newspaper. Chester rejected this line of reasoning, in language that was contrary to the conventional legal consciousness and reminiscent of Judges Cooley and Dunne, stating that "vigilance would not have prevented the publication" and therefore "the defendant was not bound personally to investigate the truth of the item." He elaborated on the doctrine related to punitive damages: "The great weight of authority is to the effect that there can be no award of punitive or exemplary damages except upon proof either of actual malice or that the libel was recklessly or carelessly published by the defendant. . . . The plaintiff is entitled to show and to have the jury consider anything which tends to establish the existence of such malice or intensify its degree, and . . . on the other hand the defendant is entitled to bring to the consideration of the jury any circumstances which legitimately tend to disprove or lessen the degree of such malice."[21]

Some crafty lawyering apparently also allowed the *Daily Gazette and Free Press* to sidestep evidentiary rules that otherwise could have undercut a libel syndicate defense. In the trial, a lawyer for the newspaper asked Oakley how many times she had been a witness in such cases, and whether it was more than a dozen. "No, sir" was her reply, but then "in response to further questions along this line, testified that she had been a witness twice in Rochester and once in Scranton; that she also had been a witness in Newark, New Orleans, St. Louis, Topeka, Cincinnati, Toledo, Charleston and in Buffalo, and then said perhaps she had been a witness a dozen times."[22] On appeal, Oakley argued that the meager six-cent award was the result of the jury being made aware of her other suits, among other factors.[23] Judge Chester ruled that the cross-examination at trial was not improper, accepting an outcome that was in keeping with the purpose of the libel syndicate defense, if not its rationale. Chester wrote that although "the rule is well settled that a defendant cannot show in mitigation of damages that the plaintiff has commenced actions against other papers for publishing the same libel," the trial court did nothing improper in allowing the newspaper's lawyer to correct Oakley when she said she had taken the stand in fewer than a dozen similar libel cases. "If the jury inferred from these facts that these other actions were libel suits, and that still others brought by the plaintiff were pending, because of the number of times she had been sworn as a witness, the inference did not arise because of any violation of the rule of evidence," Chester wrote.[24]

Oakley's status as a celebrity played a key role in her cases at every level, in the court of law and public opinion, offering an insight into how the social negotiation of the idea of a report influenced the legal consciousness surrounding the cases. In contrast to the way today's libel law disadvantages people who wield political or cultural power, Oakley's celebrity status was generally seen as a benefit in her cases against the press. One question, unique among the serial libel cases, was the element of identification: whether Annie Oakley, whose legal name was Annie Butler, could sue over a newspaper story that used her stage name and not her real name. Most courts ruled that because she was widely known for her unusual talent, Annie Butler could be identified as Annie Oakley. For example, the *Metropolis* of Jacksonville, Florida, argued that its allegedly libelous report did not identify the plaintiff, and that her complaint did not sufficiently "show on its face that the defamatory words were published of and concerning the plaintiff, Mrs. Frank E. Butler."[25] The 5th Circuit U.S. Court of Appeals rejected the *Metropolis*'s claim because Oakley had presented sufficient evidence showing that "the publication not only refers to the plaintiff by a name by which she was known, but that it refers to her vocation and skill, both of a kind unusual with women."[26] The *Wilmington* (Delaware) *Every Evening* argued that a verdict for $3,600 should be overturned because the trial judge failed to instruct the jury that the defendant newspaper "must have actually intended [the defamatory story] to refer or apply to the plaintiff," and further contended that proof that "ordinary readers . . . believe[d] that it referred to her" should not be sufficient to find in favor of Oakley.[27] The 3rd Circuit U.S. Court of Appeals rejected the *Every Evening*'s argument, finding instead that "it was competent for the jury to find, and we may add that we think they were justified in finding, that the plaintiff was the person meant in the publication in question."[28]

On the other hand, the Supreme Court of Virginia upheld a jury's finding in favor of the Richmond *News Leader* over Oakley's appeal challenging the trial court's instructions to the jurors that if they believed the evidence showed "that the article . . . did not refer to the plaintiff," and that the article in question was not likely to lead those who knew Oakley to believe it described her, "then they must find for the defendant." After a lengthy explanation of the confusing situation involving the woman jailed in Chicago and her claim to be Annie Oakley, Justice James Keith wrote that the "evidence wholly negatives actual malice." Keith added an interesting aside, incorporating his broader views about an acceptable journalistic report. "It is by a reasonable enforcement of the law and not by its harsh and strained construction that the best interests of society are [served]. . . . It is the business of a newspaper to give news. The public demands it, and it is a condition of its existence, and we cannot discover from this evidence any ground whatever upon which to rest a claim for damages against the defendant," Keith wrote.[29] Such an instance of mistaken identity should not trigger liability for a newspaper, the court ruled, because it interfered with the institution's broad social mandate to report the news.

Oakley's celebrity also drove robust discussion of her cases in the court of public opinion. Some reports about the trials, and particularly Oakley's appearances on the witness stand, were both complimentary and framed by gender. Stories contrasted the smiling performer who pranced around Buffalo Bill's arena with the woman who appeared in court, a "cultured lady in every respect," who was conservatively dressed and whose voice was "well modulated and low" and whose features were "refined and almost classical."[30] Members of the public also defended Oakley in writing to newspapers, an outpouring of support that indicated that those facing lawsuits were unlikely to meet jurors who shared their view of an acceptable journalistic report. In his 1910 letter to *Forest and Stream,* Frank Butler offered "a word of thanks to the shooting papers and sportsmen of America, who not only helped to win out, but when the article was published, first, came to her aid with strong editorials and hundreds of letters, all of which cheered and encouraged" Oakley.[31]

The Oakley suits prompted familiar strategic advice from the trade press and newspapers. The trade papers continued to encourage papers to "fight every libel suit to the last ditch," as *Editor and Publisher* put it.[32] The advice rested on the principle that linked commercial concerns to legal strategy in previous cases: juries tended to side with newspapers, and taking a strong legal stance rather than capitulating to settlement demands discouraged other plaintiffs. The *American Printer,* in a 1905 editorial, did not mention the Oakley cases directly, but argued that the press largely had itself to blame for "the current existence of a horde of dishonest, tenth-rate lawyers" who created a "false economy of money time and labor" by blackmailing newspapers.[33] In the Oakley cases, however, there was evidence that the conventional wisdom—that fighting the cases in a trial was less costly than settling them—did not necessarily hold true. From the available record, Oakley's average jury award was larger than the average settlement amount, which was the opposite of the Palmer cases.[34] When attorney fees are factored in along with the uncertainty of a jury trial, the Oakley cases might have offered a good exception to the fight-it-out rule, rather than further proof to support it.

Trade publications like the *Fourth Estate* also continued to argue that libel doctrine was unjust because it limited newspapers' opportunities to prove that libel was accidental and placed a burden on them to thoroughly check every fact they republished from other sources. A lengthy description of the *Scranton Truth*'s 1904 trial, for example, explained that the newspaper's lawyers resigned themselves to a verdict in favor of Oakley when it became clear that the judge would uphold the traditional evidentiary standards. The jury's $900 award "was not a surprise to the defense, as they had no law to sustain their contentions and unfortunately were without any evidence except what they managed to draw from the plaintiff in their favor while she was under cross-examination."[35] The appellate record in the Oakley cases provided further evidence that newspapers remained unlikely to persuade a judge to recognize a wire service defense or libel syndicate rule at trial or on appeal, in state or federal courts.

The Oakley cases demonstrate how legal risk had coalesced at the intersection of professional journalistic standards, social expectations for news, technology, and libel doctrine at the turn of the twentieth century. Some editors and reporters sought and failed to properly vet the bad news about Annie Oakley, but others received and republished it widely with no fact-checking because, as the *Cincinnati Post*'s telegraph editor explained to an Ohio court, "it was an interesting news item because of the celebrity of the person involved."[36] Indeed, celebrity was a key facet in Oakley's serial libel cases, likely contributing to the press's inability to convince courts to see how either their important social role or viable business model should be interpreted to provide legal protection for harmful mistakes. It was Oakley's prominence that led newspapers to republish the story far and wide, as they sought to serve the public's interest and their own economic interest by spotlighting the foibles of prominent people—a cornerstone of the turn-of-the-century idea of a report.

Oakley's celebrity was also her key motivation to litigate aggressively, as her reputation was central to her success as a performer. Her sympathetic story as a plaintiff wrongly subjected to bad publicity due to an egregious error helped juries translate ideas about a socially acceptable journalistic report into damage awards that reached into the tens of thousands of dollars. Even for journalists who weren't targeted by Oakley's libel suits, the cases vivified more than any previous crusade the way professional values that prioritized sensationalism, business practices that relied on speed as a competitive value, and a legal doctrine that rarely forgave defamatory errors delineated the press's social role while delimiting their legal privileges.

TABLE 2: The American Printer's List of Oakley's Suits

The list is edited for formatting, style, and clarity but otherwise is as it appeared in Louis Stotesbury, "The Famous 'Annie Oakley' Libel Suits," *American Printer* 40, no. 6 (August 1905): 533.

| PAPER | DAMAGES CLAIMED (DOLLARS) |
|---|---|
| *New York Daily News* | 25,000 |
| *Rochester* (New York) *Herald* | 25,000 |
| *Rochester* (New York) *Union and Advertiser* | 25,000 |
| *Rochester* (New York) *Times* | 25,000 |
| *Elmira* (New York) *Gazette* | 25,000 |
| *Brooklyn* (New York) *Standard Union* | 25,000 |
| *Dunkirk* (New York) *Herald* | 25,000 |
| *Boston* (Massachusetts) *Traveler* | 25,000 |
| *Boston* (Massachusetts) *Journal* | 25,000 |
| *Boston* (Massachusetts) *Advertiser* | 25,000 |
| *Boston* (Massachusetts) *Herald* | 25,000 |
| *Lowell* (Massachusetts) *Citizen* | 25,000 |
| *Bridgeport* (Connecticut) *Telegram* | 10,000 |
| *Pittsburgh* (Pennsylvania) *Leader* | 25,000 |
| *Philadelphia* (Pennsylvania) *Press* | 50,000 |
| *Scranton* (Pennsylvania) *Truth* | 10,000 |
| *Trenton* (New Jersey) *True American* | 25,000 |
| *Cincinnati* (Ohio) *Enquirer* | 25,000 |
| *Cincinnati* (Ohio) *Post* | 25,000 |
| *Toledo* (Ohio) *Times and News Bee* | 75,000 |
| *Cleveland* (Ohio) *Press* | 10,000 |
| *Cleveland* (Ohio) *World* | 10,000 |
| *Dayton* (Ohio) *Journal* | 5,000 |
| *Dayton* (Ohio) *Press* | 15,000 |
| *Dayton* (Ohio) *Herald* | 5,000 |
| *Chicago* (Illinois) *American* | 25,000 |
| *Chicago* (Illinois) *Examiner* | 25,000 |
| *St. Louis* (Missouri) *Star* | 20,000 |
| *St. Louis* (Missouri) *Chronicle* | 10,000 |
| *St. Louis* (Missouri) *Globe-Democrat* | 20,000 |
| *Des Moines* (Iowa) *News* | 35,000 |

*(continued on next page)*

TABLE 2 *(continued)*

| PAPER | DAMAGES CLAIMED (DOLLARS) |
|---|---|
| *Des Moines* (Iowa) *Capital* | 35,000 |
| *Des Moines* (Iowa) *Register Leader* | 35,000 |
| *Richmond* (Virginia) *News Leader* | 5,000 |
| *Savannah* (Georgia) *Morning News* | 15,000 |
| *Augusta* (Georgia) *Herald* | 15,000 |
| *New Orleans* (Louisiana) *Times-Democrat* | 25,000 |
| *Charleston* (South Carolina) *Evening Post* | 10,000 |
| *Charleston* (South Carolina) *News and Courier* | 10,000 |
| *Louisville* (Kentucky) *Evening Post* | 15,200 |
| *Washington* (D.C.) *Evening Star* | 30,000 |
| *Detroit* (Michigan) *Tribune* | 10,000 |
| *Topeka* (Kansas) *Daily State Journal* | 10,000 |
| Publishers' Press | 50,000 |
| Scripps-McRae Press Association | 30,000 |
| *New Haven Leader* | 10,000 |
| *Baltimore American* | 10,000 |
| *Baltimore News* | 10,000 |
| *Baltimore Evening Herald* | 10,000 |
| *Baltimore Sun* | 10,000 |
| TOTAL | 1,070,000 |
| The following judgments have been entered: | |
| *Rochester* (New York) *Times* | 1,000 |
| *Brooklyn* (New York) *Standard Union* | 1,500 |
| *Scranton* (Pennsylvania) *Truth* | 900 |
| *Hoboken* (New Jersey) *Observer* | 3,000 |
| *Cincinnati* (Ohio) *Enquirer* | 1,800 |
| *Cincinnati* (Ohio) *Post* | 2,500 |
| *New Orleans* (Louisiana) *Times-Democrat* | 5,000 |
| *Topeka* (Kansas) *Daily State Journal* | 1,000 |
| *Hoboken Observer* | 3,000 |
| TOTAL | 19,700 |

An additional update on the status of some of the cases, from "The Famous 'Annie Oakley' Libel Suits," *American Printer* 40, no. 6. (August 1905): 533.

"A number of other papers against whom no judgments have been recovered have settled with Mrs. Butler, by making substantial payments to her. The four Boston papers paid her $800 each, the three Des Moines (Iowa) papers $750 each, the St. Louis *Globe-Democrat* $1,250, the Cleveland *Plain Dealer* $1,000 to $1,200, the Kansas City Star $500 or $600.

"These are all the exact facts that we can give at this time in regard to the suits brot [*sic*], judgments recovered or settlements made, excepting that in the cases of the Rochester *Herald* and Rochester *Times* there were upon the trial disagreements of the jury, and in the case against the Richmond *News-Leader,* there was a verdict for the defendant. In the case of the New Orleans *Times-Democrat,* the verdict was for $7,500 and was reduced by the court to $5,000. In the case of the Cincinnati *Post,* the verdict was for $9,000, which was reduced by the court to $2,500 and appealed. The verdicts of $1,000 against the Topeka State *Journal* and Pittsburg *Leader* have been paid. In the case of the Hoboken *Observer* an appeal from judgment was taken. In the case against the Cincinnati *Inquirer* [*sic*], a motion for a new trial was made, but we have not been advised of the result."

CHAPTER 6

# *BAD NEWS AND THE BAD TENDENCY TEST*

–···/·–/–··/ –·/·/·––/···/

## THE LIMITS OF LIBEL DOCTRINE

The serial libel cases forced a reconsideration of how a legal doctrine that had developed to protect individual reputation and ensure publisher propriety should apply to an industry that increasingly valued speed, scale, accuracy, and sensationalism. Fundamentally, the cases played a key role in the social negotiation of what constituted an acceptable journalistic report in the public sphere. Debate in courtrooms and the court of public opinion focused on whether the legal rules should be refashioned to protect newspapers in their role as information disseminators when their reliance on the telegraph and news wire services in that role led to false and harmful mistakes. Many of the newspaper defendants targeted by the suits asserted the need for a wire service defense: a claim that their regular use of a normally trustworthy wire service in publishing the defamatory report should limit the punitive or exemplary damages they owed the plaintiff. Newspapers also argued that evidence of other suits filed by the plaintiff for the same alleged libel should be made available to the jury in the form of a libel syndicate defense, which would result in a more fair and informed damage award in consideration of the plaintiff's other lawsuits.

The wire service and libel syndicate defenses were specific strategies reflecting a broader reconceptualization of the role the daily newspaper served in democratic society, focusing on the speed and efficiency of information dissemination. The press argued that accidentally inaccurate reports should not be treated the same as intentional or malicious lies (particularly when a prompt correction, retraction, or apology was made), that republication or repetition of a libelous report should not be treated the same as the original publication when so many newspapers relied on the wires for so much of their news, and that judicial standards should incorporate the informational function of the press in balancing the rights and responsibilities of defendants and plaintiffs. The press's arguments were an attempt to intervene in the established legal consciousness surrounding libel, which favored protecting an individual's right to maintain their good name regardless of the practices, processes, or intentions of the publisher who defamed them. Moreover, it reflected an idea of a report that valued speed and sensationalism as meeting the expectations of modern readers and the business interests of the news industry.

The Smith and Rutherford cases showed newspapers that serial libel suits could represent a serious pitfall to their use of wire service news. Judges were unlikely to accept the wire service or libel syndicate defenses, and jurors, when offended by a newspapers' willingness to publish a salacious story without first confirming its truth, were likely to award large damages. In the Palmer and de Freitas cases, journalists faced a growing body of case law that rejected the wire service and libel syndicate defenses and also growing evidence that serial libel plaintiffs like Palmer could be thwarted when newspapers fought libel suits rather than settling them, relying on the likelihood that sympathetic local juries would favor hometown newspapers over an unknown and possibly unharmed interloper. The Oakley cases, however, offered the opposite lesson, as the celebrity persona of Annie Oakley drove both the widespread publication of the original false story as well as the famous performer's success in the courtroom as a witness. In fact, juries in New Orleans and Cincinnati were sympathetic enough to Oakley's case that they awarded her damage amounts that the presiding trial judges later determined were too large.[1] While these differences may have contributed to a perception that juries' verdicts were, as Holmes put it, "more or less accidental" and could be subject to distraction or emotion, it also reflects nuance developing in the relationship between social consciousness surrounding the idea of a report and the law, where contextual factors like intrusiveness, harm, anonymity, and fame could all play a role in the outcomes of libel cases.[2]

Overall, newspapers were mostly unsuccessful in convincing judges to limit their responsibility to plaintiffs based on a rationale that favored the public need for news over the rights of individuals to maintain an unsullied reputation. Judges were also generally unwilling to curtail the relatively free rein of juries to punish publishers they considered to have overstepped the bounds of decency. The bad tendency test for bad news, deployed through the strict liability doctrine, prevailed across twenty-eight appellate decisions in serial libel cases between 1891 and 1907. In ten of those twenty-eight decisions, courts explicitly rejected the wire service or libel syndicate defense.[3] But there were key exceptions, too. In four decisions, judges ruled in favor of the press, either explicitly accepting a wire service or libel syndicate defense or more generally applying an analytical approach that acknowledged a newspaper's role as an informer of the public on a broad range of issues and suggested that punishments for such inevitable accidents of the industrialized marketplace should be limited.[4]

Newspapers' assertion of the wire service defense succeeded most notably in the *Chicago Herald*'s appeal of Juliette Smith's $15,000 verdict in 1894, in Tyndale Palmer's suit against the *Buffalo Illustrated Express* in 1898, and in Annie Oakley's appeal for a new trial after being awarded six cents in damages against the *Elmira Daily Gazette and Free Press* in 1907. In each of those cases, appellate judges acknowledged the press's broad argument that libel doctrine could disproportionately punish newspapers for mistakes that occurred in the course of publishing stories about matters of public interest. In the *Chicago Herald* case, Judge Dunne argued that the trial court improperly placed all the responsibility for the error on the newspaper and disregarded any responsibility Smith or Rutherford might have to minimize their own harm, despite knowing that newspapers could not possibly verify every item they publish.[5] This rationale not only favored the modern press but also reflected some of the emerging legal thinking about diffuse negligence in an industrialized and accident-prone society, applying it to the place of wire services in the news industry.[6] In the *Illustrated Express* case, an intermediate appellate court in New York ruled that it was appropriate for the newspaper to introduce evidence that the newspaper had received the story about Palmer's alleged fraud from a wire service and published it "in good faith and in reliance upon its accuracy and truth" as was "common with many other newspapers throughout the country."[7] In the *Daily Gazette and Free Press* case, Judge Chester argued that it was germane to the assessment of damages for the jury to consider whether the newspaper should be expected to verify a wire service story before publishing it, as it could help explain whether the newspaper acted with malice.[8]

The judges that accepted the logic of the wire service defense were outliers, however. In the majority of appeals where the wire service defense was asserted or discussed, judges held firm to the traditional strict liability doctrine that required newspapers to assume complete responsibility for what they published, and did not allow those defendants to mitigate their damages by way of an explanation of their standard business practices or their role as disseminators of information. Judges did not necessarily reject the principle that newspapers gathered news from all corners of the globe and delivered it to their readers with speed and efficiency; they simply argued that libel doctrine did not allow that fact—or the idea of a report that it encompassed—to offer an excuse or defense in a libel suit. They cited common law standards of liability that favored an individual's right to protect his or her reputation and considered newspapers' tendency to trust wire service stories without verification to be irrelevant, if not damning, for juries calculating damages.[9]

Meanwhile, on the libel syndicate defense front, success was rarely the result of an appellate court agreeing with newspapers that jurors should mitigate damages based on the scale of a plaintiff's legal crusade. More often, judges ruled that when a jury may have taken a libel syndicate into account in calculating damages, that fact did not justify overturning an otherwise properly decided verdict. For example, when Palmer appealed the nominal damages he was awarded in his 1898 suit against the *Buffalo Illustrated Express* as unfairly small, the court argued that he assumed a risk that his case might be undermined when he admitted into evidence letters that he wrote to the newspaper, some of which noted that he had filed other suits against other papers.[10] (A higher court disagreed and sent the case back to trial, however.)[11] Similarly, in Oakley's appeal for a new trial against the *Elmira Daily Gazette and Free Press* in 1907, the court ruled that although the number of a plaintiff's total suits for the same libel was not admissible as relevant evidence, the fact that it came up in a cross-examination and could therefore have led the jury to infer that Oakley was pursuing many suits elsewhere was not a legal error that required returning the case to trial. The libel syndicate defense usually failed because, as with the wire service defense, it cut against well-established doctrine that judges were unwilling to reverse. The standard was succinctly said to be "talebearers are as bad as talemakers," and the fact that there were dozens or even hundreds of talebearers who repeated a libelous tale should not limit the damages a jury chose to award in any single case.[12]

Thus, while one or two appellate judges were willing to accept the logic or outcome of the wire service or libel syndicate defense in each of the serial libel cases, most courts deferred to the prevailing doctrine of the day: strict liability for libel and limited opportunities to mitigate damages by undermining the presumption of malice. "A person publishes libellous [*sic*] matter at his peril," as Justice Holmes said.[13] Judges' legal rationales reflected a legal consciousness that prioritized the need to protect the reputations of otherwise defenseless and blameless individuals, as well as the public sphere, from the spread of false and sensational news stories. Judges generally saw no reason to extend a special privilege to the press, even where a newspaper could argue that a libel occurred as a result of an honest mistake or that the amount of damages it owed to the plaintiff should be weighed against his or her other suits for the same libel. While other areas of tort law at the turn of the twentieth century struggled to draw a line between private law and public policy and tended toward subjective analyses of fault and malice in the interest of fairness amid accidental harm, libel doctrine remained planted on firm, traditional ground. Judges in the serial libel cases argued in favor of the public policy benefits of holding newspapers strictly accountable: "social happiness and domestic peace,"[14] ensured by an objective standard that was unconcerned with whether a libel was accidental or malicious.

Looking at the appellate record alone in the serial libel cases could wrongly lead to the conclusion that because the wire service and libel syndicate defenses failed to get a strong foothold in doctrine, the cases were disastrous for the press. This was not the case, however, and the reasons relate to the nuances of the debate around the forms and practices that made up an acceptable journalistic report. In some instances, members of the public—jurors—appeared to agree with publishers that a degree of protection should be extended to the press, even if this was not a view held by most appellate judges. This appeared to be particularly true when, such as in the Palmer cases, jurors considered the story at issue or its widespread distribution and republication not to be an especially intrusive or egregious mischaracterization, because the plaintiff did not appear to have suffered serious harm in the locale he or she was suing, or because his or her social status did not warrant a large damage award that compensated loss to reputation or punished a careless or malicious newspaper. Interestingly, Judge Cooley had all but predicted the relationship between social and legal consciousness on questions of acceptable journalism, technology, and libel in his 1868 treatise on constitutional law, in which he argued that "whatever view the law may take," "public sentiment" does not necessarily brand a publisher a libelous villain for accidentally publishing an inaccurate telegraph dispatch.[15]

The contrast between the relatively small damage amounts juries awarded to Palmer and the larger amounts they awarded to Smith, Rutherford, and Oakley also suggests that jurors viewed these cases through a lens similar to Cooley's when distinguishing among the social statuses of plaintiffs and the topics of the offending stories. In the 1883 edition of his treatise, Cooley argued that libel law should recognize the differences among "private individuals" who "only challenge . . . public criticism when [their] conduct becomes or threatens to be injurious to others" and "public characters [who] invite it at all times."[16] While there is scanty evidence on the specific instructions given to jurors in the serial libel cases, it is reasonable to suggest that jurors saw Smith and Rutherford as something like "private individuals" who did not "challenge public criticism" and thus deserved punitive damages, and Palmer as a private individual whose (alleged) conduct invited such criticism and thus did not deserve such damages. As for Oakley—surely a "public character"—jurors may have seen fit to award punitive damages because, as Cooley wrote and appellate judges in the serial libel cases echoed, "a false and injurious publication made in a public journal for sensation and increase of circulation is unquestionably in a legal sense malicious."[17]

The financial implications of the serial libel cases were also not existentially catastrophic for individual defendants or the press as a whole. Few newspapers, if any, were forced to fold as a result of these cases or any libel suits during the turn of the twentieth century.[18] Nevertheless, the cases raised the danger of self-censorship: a "chilling effect" on key aspects of newspapers' professional practices.[19] As documented in the trade press, increased fear about libel suits led publishers to sink more resources into legal defense and be more vigilant against accidental falsehoods, especially via wire services. Of course, this was the intended outcome of a libel doctrine based on strict liability with few opportunities to mitigate damages. But newspapers were thereby forced to choose between competing fully in a marketplace that favored a broad range of news—from politics to the follies and foibles of regular folks—or printing more carefully and soberly, restricting their contribution to the public sphere on clear matters of public importance and potentially losing circulation—and advertising dollars—to more rambunctious competitors. Thus, while press defendants and advocates did not argue that the First Amendment required recognition of a wire service or libel syndicate defense, legal consciousness within the industry reflected a need for a doctrine that was more just and practical in view of the press's professional identity and its economic reliance on telegraph-based wire service news. Appellate courts largely rejected this view, but it appears that the public was prepared to make some room in the concept of press freedom for news stories that were false and caused reputational harm, but were not malicious or outrageous.

Indeed, during the era of the serial libel cases, the press found lawmakers more receptive than judges in some states to the idea that the law should ease the burden on newspapers that swiftly and prominently apologized for their mistakes. But the statutes also clashed with another fundamental problem for press freedom and the public sphere: whether they improperly placed the free speech rights of newspapers above those of other libel defendants.

## TABLE 3: Appellate Rulings in the Serial Libel Cases

The rulings are listed in roughly chronological order by date of first appellate opinion. In some cases, amount sued for or amount awarded was not reported in an appellate opinion or in news or trade press coverage.

| PLAINTIFF | DEFENDANT (NEWSPAPER) | STATE; APPELLATE JURISDICTION | AMOUNT SUED FOR (IF KNOWN) | JURY'S VERDICT | AMOUNT AWARDED (IF KNOWN |
|---|---|---|---|---|---|
| Rutherford | Morning Journal Assoc. (*New York Morning Journal*) | New York; 2nd U.S. Cir. | | For plaintiff | |
| Smith | Sun Publishing Co. (*New York Sun*) | New York; 2nd U.S. Cir. | | For Plaintiff | $7,500 |
| Smith | J. N. Matthews (*Buffalo Morning Express* and *Illustrated Express*) | New York; State | | For Plaintiff | $4,000 |
| Smith | *Chicago Herald* | Illinois; State | | For Plaintiff | $15,000 |
| | | | | | |
| Palmer | E. P. Bailey & Co. (*Utica Observer*) | New York; State | $25,000 | For Plaintiff | $25 |
| Palmer | New York News Publishing Co. (*New York Daily News*) | New York; State | $25,000 | For Plaintiff | $7,500 |
| Palmer | The Leader Publishing Co. (*Pittsburgh Leader*) | Pennsylvania; State | $50,000 | For Plaintiff | 6.25 cents |
| | | | | | |
| Oakley | Carter and Russell Publishing Co. (*Jacksonville Metropolis*) | Florida; 5th U.S. Cir. | | For Plaintiff | |
| Oakley | Times-Democrat Publishing Co. (*New Orleans Times-Democrat*) | Louisiana; 5th U.S. Cir. | $25,000 | For Plaintiff | $7,500 by jur reduced to $5,000 on appeal |
| Oakley | Post Publishing Co. (*Cincinnati Post*) | Ohio; 6th U.S. Cir. | $25,000 | For Plaintiff | $9,000 by ju reduced to $2,500 on appeal |
| Oakley | News-Leader Co. (Richmond *News Leader*) | Virginia; State | $5,000 | For Defendant | |

| PPELLATE OPINION CITATIONS | APPELLATE OUTCOME |
|---|---|
| utherford v. Morning Journal Asso., 47 F. 487 :.C.D.N.Y. 1891); Morning Journal Asso. v. Ruth- ford, 51 F. 513 (2d Cir. N.Y. 1892) | Morning Journal's motion to set aside "excessive" verdict was rejected. |
| nith v. Sun Pub. Co., 50 F. 399 (C.C.D.N.Y. 92); Smith v. Sun Printing & Pub. Asso., 55 F. o (2d Cir. N.Y. 1893) | Sun's motion for a new trial asserting various errors by trial court was rejected. |
| nith v. Matthews, 6 Misc. 162, 27 N.Y.S. 120, 1893 N.Y. Super. Ct. 1893); Smith v. Matthews, 9 Misc. 27, 29 N.Y.S. 1058 (N.Y. Super. Ct. 1894); Smith v. latthews, 46 N.E. 164 (1897) | Matthews's motion for a new trial asserting various errors by trial court was rejected. |
| nith v. Chicago Herald, Chicago Legal News, l. 26, no. 40, p. 317–318, June 2, 1894; Albany Law urnal, vol. 50, p. 23, July 7, 1894 | *Herald*'s motion to set aside "excessive" verdict was granted. |
| | |
| lmer v. E. P. Bailey & Co., 12 A.D. 6 (Sup. Ct. Y. App. Div. 1896); Palmer v. E. P. Bailey & Co., A.D. 630 (N.Y. App. Div. 1897); lmer v. E. P. Bailey & Co., 33 A.D. 642 (N.Y. pp. Div. 1898) | Palmer's motion for a new trial, based on admission of evidence of his "pecuniary standing," was granted. |
| lmer v. New York News Pub. Co., 31 A.D. 210 N.Y. App. Div. 1898); Palmer v. New York News ıb. Co., 158 N.Y. 664 (N.Y. 1899) | New York News's motion for a new trial, seeking to assert "wire service" defense and "libel syndicate" defense, was rejected. |
| lmer v. The Leader Publishing Company 7 Pa. per. 594 (Super. Ct. Penn. 1898) | Palmer's motion for a new trial, arguing that nominal damages were insufficient, was rejected. |
| | |
| ıtler v. Carter & Russell Pub. Co., 135 F. 69 (5th r. Fla. 1905) | Carter and Russell's argument that Oakley failed to show the libelous statements identified her was rejected. |
| mes-Democrat Pub. Co. v. Mozee, 136 F. 761 th Cir. La. 1905) | Times-Democrat's argument that Louisiana law prohib- ited Oakley to recover damages for "shame, disgrace, and mental suffering" was rejected. |
| st Pub. Co. v. Butler, 137 F. 723 (6th Cir. Ohio 05) | Post's argument that Ohio's retraction statute should undercut Oakley's suit was rejected. |
| ıtler v. News-Leader Co., 104 Va. 1 (Va. 1905) | Oakley's argument that the trial court's finding that the libel did not identify her was an error was rejected. (*continued on next page*) |

TABLE 3 *(continued)*

| PLAINTIFF | DEFENDANT (NEWSPAPER) | STATE; APPELLATE JURISDICTION | AMOUNT SUED FOR (IF KNOWN) | JURY'S VERDICT | AMOUNT AWARDED (IF KNOW |
|---|---|---|---|---|---|
| Oakley | Hoboken Printing and Publishing Co. (*Hoboken Observer*) | New Jersey; State | | For Plaintiff | $3,000 |
| Oakley | Every Evening Printing Co. (*Wilmington Every Evening*) | Delaware; 3rd U.S. Cir. | | For Plaintiff | $3,600 |
| Oakley | Evening Leader Co. (*New Haven Evening Leader*) | Connecticut; 2nd U.S. Cir. | $10,000 | For Plaintiff | |
| Oakley | Evening Post Publishing Co. (*Charleston Evening Post* and *News and Courier*) | South Carolina; 4th U.S. Cir. | $10,000 each | | |
| Oakley | Gazette Co. (*Elmira Daily Gazette* and *Free Press*) | New York; State | 25,000 | For Plaintiff | 6 cents |

| PPELLATE OPINION CITATIONS | APPELLATE OUTCOME |
|---|---|
| utler v. Hoboken Printing & Publ’g Co., 73 J.L. 45 (Sup. Ct. 1905) | Hoboken Printing & Publishing’s argument in favor of admission of a “libel syndicate” defense was rejected, but motion for new trial was granted because Oakley failed to establish connection between the libel and loss of earnings and physical distress. |
| utler v. Every Evening Printing Co., 140 F. 934 C.C.D. Del. 1905); Every Evening Printing Co. v. utler, 144 F. 916 (3d Cir. Del. 1906) | Every Evening’s motion for a new trial asserting various errors by trial court, including evidence of mistaken identity, was rejected. |
| utler v. Evening Leader Co., 134 F. 994 (C.C.D. onn. 1905); Evening Leader Co. v. Butler, 151 F. 20 (2d Cir. Conn. 1907) | Evening Leader’s argument that mistaken identity should constitute a “complete justification” was rejected. |
| utler v. Evening Post Pub. Co., 148 F. 821 4th Cir. S.C. 1906) | Oakley’s motion for a new trial, based on errors in the jury selection process of two consolidated cases, was granted. |
| utler v. Gazette Co., 119 A.D. 767 (N.Y. App. Div. 07) | Oakley’s motion for a new trial, asserting trial court errors, including allowing “wire service” and “libel syndicate” defenses, was rejected. |

CHAPTER 7

# *RETRACTION STATUTES*

## AN ALTERNATE ROUTE TO PROTECTION

In 1905, the Sixth Circuit U.S. Court of Appeals heard the *Cincinnati Post*'s appeal of a $2,500 verdict in favor of Annie Oakley for the infamous story about drugs and destitution. At the center of the *Post*'s appeal was an Ohio law, passed in 1900, that limited a libel plaintiff's ability to collect damages when the defendant publisher made a prompt, prominent, and complete retraction of the libelous statement upon the plaintiff's request, and showed that the publication "was made in good faith, through mistake of fact, but with reasonable ground for believing that the statements therein contained were true."[1] The *Post* argued that the statute precluded Oakley's damage award, since the newspaper published a correction to the original story, undercutting her argument that the libel was published maliciously. Oakley argued that the statute could not apply because she never requested a retraction from the *Post,* and even if it did apply the statute violated the Ohio constitution's guarantee of due process by denying her an opportunity to seek a remedy for the libel.[2] The federal court sided with Oakley, and in its ruling said it chose the only interpretation that would not invalidate the statute as unconstitutional: when a libel plaintiff demanded and received a retraction (which was not the case here), "he . . . consents that he be restricted, in addition to the reparation thus afforded, to a recovery of special damages where he can show actual malice. Under this interpretation he is not deprived of any constitutional right because he consents to the application of the new law to his case. If he does not consent, he still has the remedy under the old law."[3]

Although the outcome of the case was not favorable to the *Post,* it was good news for the press of Ohio because it preserved a controversial piece of legislation intended to protect diligent and well-meaning newspaper publishers from burdensome libel suits. The Ohio law was one of seventeen libel laws passed across the country between 1885 and 1915.[4] Now commonly called "retraction statutes," they generally limited the damages a plaintiff could recover when the publisher of an alleged libel printed a retraction and presented evidence showing an absence of malice. The debate surrounding the laws offers another look at how the legal consciousness of libel law and the idea of a report were socially negotiated at the time of the serial libel suits. The emerging state and national journalism trade associations lobbied hard for retraction laws, and hailed them as welcome relief from a constant threat to the press's ability to publish the news.[5] But critics on the bench and at the bar argued that the new laws improperly favored the press and denied a rightful remedy to people who were harmed by sloppy and sensational reporting. During the serial libel era, high courts in four states struck down newly passed retraction statutes, and the legislatures of two states repealed their statutes within a few years of creating them.[6] In fact, the Supreme Court of Ohio struck down that state's retraction statute six years after the *Post* decision.[7]

In all, newspapers and press advocates were more successful in state legislatures than in the courts in their fight to limit the potential damage of serial libel cases, but marginally so. Of the seventeen statutes passed between 1885 and 1915, eleven avoided legislative repeal or judicial rejection, offering some breathing space in those states to deliver news to the public with high speed and broad scope, without the threat of a costly libel verdict on every page. The key obstacles to passing and maintaining the retraction statutes were questions about whether the press should benefit from laws that seemed to protect the rampant and freewheeling use of the telegraphic wire services and whether press rights should be elevated above the rights of individuals who were harmed, even if accidentally. On the other hand, the modest success of the organized press's lobbying efforts demonstrated the power of organization and unity that the press could use to advance its interests, even when those interests created tension in the relationship with the public and when the interests' connection to a broader social good was less than clear. This success showed that the organized, institutional press could wield influence over legal consciousness and signaled a gradual move toward a more press-friendly libel climate.

Press associations took on the libel problem quickly after they were established, and with vigor, but lawyers and law journal editors were suspicious of efforts to create special libel protections for the press. The rift over whether the acceptable idea of a journalistic report should include occasional mistakes made at high speed and at large scale, and how the law should respond, was evident early. At the National Editorial Association's second-ever annual meeting in Cincinnati in February 1886, association president Benjamin Herbert argued in his keynote address that in the modern age, "the necessity of the rapid collection of news should relieve the newspaper from the antiquated rule" of libel law.[8] In August that same year, American Bar Association president William Allen Butler derided Michigan's new retraction statute, in an address summarizing nationwide legislative trends at the ABA's annual meeting. Butler called the law a "tender consideration of newspaper publishers" that "would seem rather to be a premium upon scrutiny and care after libel, to avoid punishment, rather than . . . to prevent its utterance." In July 1888 the *Albany Law Journal* put a finer point on the criticism: "It is like the wolves demanding to have the lambs muzzled."[9]

At the American Newspaper Publishers Association's (ANPA) third annual convention, in 1890, founding member William H. Brearly presided over a discussion titled: "What are the best methods to secure Uniform Libel Laws in the States?"[10] Given ANPA members' focus on business interests, it is unsurprising that their complaints and concerns stemmed from the threat that libel suits posed to their bottom lines. However, the discussion also raised several themes that would continually emerge from the professional associations' discussions of libel law reform: a strategic focus on lobbying state legislatures using model statute language, a belief that lawyers posed a challenge to reform efforts due to their professional stake and political influence in plaintiff-friendly libel laws, and concerns that by favoring the press as a specific class, retraction statutes would be disfavored by lawmakers and judges.

The press associations' lobbying strategy grew out of researching the issue. In 1889 the New York Press Association assigned E. H. Butler of the *Buffalo News* and Carroll Smith of the *Syracuse Journal* to report on reform efforts in New York and other states. Butler's report, "The Progress of Libel-Law Reform," argued that such efforts were "a worthy campaign" needed to protect "the greatest engine of modern civilization." Smith, on behalf of the association's legislative committee, proposed a law that would allow a strong defense when a libelous item was retracted, limit plaintiffs' compensation to actual damages, and eliminate the law's presumption of defendant malice.[11] Butler shared his report with the NEA as a delegate to the annual meeting in Detroit in 1889, where Herbert called it "a most elaborate and studiously prepared digest," making a strong case for libel reform across the country.[12]

The trade associations also commissioned the help of lawyers to compile reports and help strategize and energize lobbying campaigns. Attorneys E. A. Snively, from Springfield, Illinois, and Azel F. Hatch, from Chicago, provided reports to the NEA and ANPA.[13] Both were members of the press association in Illinois, where a retraction statute was adopted in 1895.[14] In providing a comprehensive synthesis on the state of libel law to the ANPA that year, Hatch linked the need for retraction statutes to a broader social concern: the need for an informed public in a democracy. "You have no right of publication inherent," Hatch explained to the newspaper publishers; "that right is justified only by the rights of the public and the benefit of the public."[15] Hatch argued that retraction statutes therefore struck a balance between the right of an individual to his or her reputation and the rights of the broader public in being informed. Snively and Hatch encouraged editors and publishers to push on with persistence, and to levy their unique position of political influence against resistance by legislators.[16]

Editors' and publishers' strategies to encourage cooperation from state legislators evolved as they encountered challenges. As early as 1890, President Brearly of the ANPA argued that lobbying efforts should utilize "the wisdom of the corporations" by publicly endorsing and supporting press-friendly legislators who would work on the newspapers' behalf. His motion was unanimously approved.[17] By 1895, however, the ANPA strategy moved lobbying efforts out of the public eye. Charles Taylor of the

*Boston Globe* explained to ANPA members that although the newspapers of Massachusetts had been working hard to change state laws, they no longer took to their editorial pages to advocate for change or excoriate the politicians who opposed it, because it seemed to harm their efforts when the bills went before the legislature. Instead, editors and publishers shared "a strong understanding that we would not print in our papers a line about the proposed law of libel; that until it was defeated or passed we would not touch it in any way, shape or matter." Taylor said publishers in Massachusetts instead told candidates that libel law reform was the only issue that interested them. "They will say [to candidates]: 'Here is the only thing we want from the Legislature, and if you want us to do anything for you[,] you have got to do this for us.'"[18]

Editors and publishers blamed opposition on self-interested legislators who worked as attorneys. In his 1889 report to the NEA, E. H. Butler warned, "If the action of one or two legislators may be taken as a sample of the sentiment and feeling which the lawyers . . . have for the members of the press, libel law reform, I fear, will be very slow."[19] In response to Brearly's 1890 prompt to discuss methods of securing reform, an ANPA member from Pennsylvania worried, "As long as the legislature is composed of attorneys and politicians, I fear there is not much hope." A member from Massachusetts blamed his state's failure to pass a retraction statute on the lawyers who profited from blackmail suits.[20] Attorneys like Snively and Hatch, who helped and supported reform efforts, were considered the exception rather than the rule. Indeed, in 1895 Hatch warned ANPA members that lawyers were "the most active source of opposition" because they wanted to continue their lawsuits against the press.[21]

A divide between city papers and country papers also concerned members of the press associations, and revealed potentially more fundamental disagreement over what journalistic forms and practices ought to be considered acceptable. At the 1890 ANPA meeting, Lewis Baker, publisher of the *St. Paul* (Minnesota) *Globe,* said that opposition to his state's retraction statute in 1887 came from "pettifogging lawyers" as well as country editors who saw frequent libel suits as "proper punishment for the larger papers."[22] The New York Press Association's long-running and unsuccessful efforts to pass a retraction statute reflected the same challenges. For example, after the legislative committee reported another failure to secure any change to the state's libel law in 1891, Carroll Smith called the "richly paid attorneys of the New York newspapers . . . the worst enemies of newspapers throughout the state." In an 1894 legislative committee report, Charles Skinner noted that when lawmakers debated a retraction statute that eventually failed, "many of the senators charged that the metropolitan press had been particularly vindictive in comments upon senators and public measures." Even A. O. Bunnell, who was largely even-handed in his authorized history of the NYPA, placed the ultimate blame for the failure to change New York's libel law on the "rich metropolitan journals who, for advertising purposes, are inclined to like libel suits, and the large class of shyster lawyers, who make it a part of their business to promote libel suits."[23]

Professional preservation may have underpinned attorney opposition to libel reform laws, but in law journal articles and ABA meeting minutes, the focus was on the laws' substance, where commentators found flaws in protecting careless news publishing practices and compromising sound libel doctrine. In 1889, the *Harvard Law Review* argued that retraction statutes "do not promote the ends of justice" given that "a man's right to reputation is as sacred as his right to life and liberty, and should be guarded as carefully." Moreover, the unsigned note argued, common law doctrine provided ample protection for "respectable" newspapers to "keep clear of libel suits while maintaining a proper fearlessness and independence in a discussion of public affairs."[24] In an 1895 speech, President James C. Carter of the ABA echoed similar confidence in the common law: "Such legislation seems of very doubtful expediency. The law of libel built up by the wisdom of jurists upon close consideration of all the forms in which reputation is liable to be assailed, is not likely to be improved by legislative action, especially such as is sought for by the modern newspaper press."[25]

Nevertheless, the press associations proposed and debated legislative language that would reflect their conception that mistakes were not malicious and undercut the plaintiff-friendly common law. In 1887, NEA president Albert Blakeslee White, publisher of the *Parkersburg State Journal* (and future governor of West Virginia), proposed that a model retraction statute be drafted and provided to state associations. "A greater service could hardly be rendered to the journalists of the country," White said.[26] The model statute was a single sentence: "[W]here alleged libelous publications are made, malice shall not be presumed unless a retraction or apology is refused to be made, or unless the circumstances surrounding the publication and its refusal to retract or apologize conclusively prove malice." The effort to officially adopt the language and pass it on to state press associations stalled, however, when the committee assigned to draft it could only agree to a more general motion that the state associations should lobby their legislatures for reform. Creating a single, suitable statute for all states was "almost or quite impossible," committee members said.[27] Butler and Smith's reports to the New York Press Association in 1889 included no proposed statutory language, but they did specify that the law should require a plaintiff to prove malice and that a retraction of the alleged libel should mitigate the damages awarded to the defendant.[28]

The Minnesota retraction statute, which was enacted in 1887 and survived a constitutional challenge in 1889,[29] was frequently cited as being a good model. It limited plaintiffs to recovering only actual damages when the defendant could present evidence that (1) the article was published in "good faith," (2) falsity was due to "a mistake or misapprehension of the facts," and (3) a correction was printed within three days of receiving notice or in the next regular issue of the publication that was equally conspicuous to the original article.[30] In 1890, the New York Press Association's legislative committee "substantially recommended . . . the Minnesota statute" with minimal changes.[31] An 1893 ANPA discussion about whether "a uniform libel law" was possible or advisable centered on the Minnesota law as a model.[32] In 1895, a resolution adopted by the International League of Press Clubs urged its members to lobby for retraction statutes in every state using model language that was virtually identical to laws adopted in Minnesota and, that year, in Indiana. In proposing the resolution, delegate John Fow invoked the constitutional guarantee of freedom of the press, arguing that reform would protect newspapers whose "duty" and "right" was to "expose public scandal, maladministration of office and violation of law."[33] Such an explicit link to the values of journalistic professional identity was quite rare in the accounts of press associations' lobbying efforts, as most of the rhetoric was practical and strategic.

Newspaper publishers' sense of their special role in democracy was more frequently found in the trade press, however, where it was argued that unjust libel laws inhibited the press's ability to keep the powerful accountable to the public. In its very first issue on March 22, 1884, the *Journalist* called for reform because, under current standards, "great frauds and great wrongs might never be redressed."[34] The *Journalist* continually reminded readers about the public value newspapers served: "The best detective we have is the newspaper, and its work has proven this."[35] In March 1897, *Newspaperdom* reprinted a Youngstown, Ohio, newspaper's claim that the series of libel suits it had fought represented "no less a question than freedom of the press in eastern Ohio."[36] In August 1898, the *Fourth Estate* excerpted part of an editorial co-written by the editor and publisher of the *Loveland* (Colorado) *Reporter* following their arrest for eleven counts of criminal libel. The editorial excoriates the accusers and valorizes the journalistic enterprise: "Libel or no libel—we are here for business: to uphold that which is just, honorable, decent and worthy: here to condemn what is lowering, indecent, false and harmful."[37] In a lengthy "year in review" piece looking back on 1897, the *Fourth Estate* observed that where legislators voted in favor of libel law reform that year, they "learned that with the vigorous and energetic newspapers watching everything they do and ready to call attention to intrusions of public right and corruption of legislative acts it is best to be as honest as it is possible for politicians to be."[38] And when the Illinois legislature decided to repeal its two-year-old reform law, the *Fourth Estate* said in June 1897 that the decision was "revenge" against the "bold" newspapers that had exposed legislative corruption.[39]

Indeed, a key challenge retraction statutes faced was tied to journalists' claims to need special protection for their social role: judges' and lawmakers' distaste for "class legislation" which singled out any group for special treatment. As part of the attempt to maintain objective standards of rule-making, jurists and legal thinkers sought to hold the line on corruption, privileges, exceptions, and exemptions that favored lobbyists and special interests through an equal playing field of property rights, exchange rules, and public order. Such thinking was reflected in Cooley's focus on acts, not motives, in tort law: "That which it is right and lawful for one man to do cannot furnish the foundation for an action in favor of another."[40] The rejection of class legislation was part of the broader project of transforming law and legislation into a science, where duties and rights were identified, categorized, and balanced with impartial predictability.[41] In the prescient 1890 discussion that reflected several themes related to press associations' reform efforts, ANPA's Brearly noted that it was the class legislation issue that led to the demise of Michigan's retraction statute, enacted in 1885 and then overturned by the state supreme court in 1888.[42] By the same token, the extent to which special legislation that benefitted the press was considered acceptable illustrated differences of opinion on the matter, such as Holmes's critique that objective legal analysis, free of public policy considerations, was impossible and perhaps even unwise.[43]

*The Advocate* rejected the notion that the press's public role required special protection in 1889. "Some change in the law of libel is highly desirable," the legal journal argued, "but most of the proposed amendments . . . lean in the wrong direction." Instead, the article argued, singling out newspapers "to exempt them from a rigid responsibility for torts" risked emboldening editors toward carelessness and rumormongering. "The power of the journal over the individual's comfort . . . is increasing, and ought to be diminished," the article argued. Oddly, the article supported a Wisconsin bill that covered most of what the press associations were pushing for; it limited libel plaintiffs to actual damages, prevented lawsuits where plaintiffs did not first demand a retraction, and forbade libel suits where lawyers worked on a contingent fee basis. "This seems to be as much as newspapers should ask or expect," the article concluded.[44]

The editors of the *Albany Law Journal* had grown exasperated by how frequently they felt compelled to argue against the retraction bills proposed in the New York legislature in 1889. "We . . . do not care to reiterate," they wrote, before providing a detailed takedown of the most recent proposal.[45] An 1893 article attacked the latest New York bill, which closely resembled Minnesota's law. The article clearly staked out a claim on what its authors considered an acceptable journalistic report, arguing that the concept of "good faith," which when proven by the defendant could limit a plaintiff's claim to damages, was "too vague," as it could allow publishers a broad excuse for failing to confirm second-hand information.[46] It also argued that there were flaws in the ways retraction statutes limited damages. They did not allow for "just compensation for unmerited anguish caused by the false publication," for example, and denied compensation to people who could *only* show harm to their to reputation, not in their business or occupation, such as a woman accused of being unchaste or a clergyman accused of being impious.[47] Placing a burden of proof of damages on such plaintiffs, when "any one can see that they must have suffered damage," was "unwise," the editors wrote.[48] The *American Law Review* was more blunt in its ridicule of the Illinois retraction statute passed in 1895. Retractions are "notoriously inefficient for the purpose intended" since they do not reach all the readers of the original statement, the article argued, adding that the new law "ought to be known as the 'encouragement of libel act.'"[49]

The opposition was not universal, however. An 1897 article in the *Albany Law Journal* noted that "the views and opinions of leading jurists and lawyers differ quite radically as to what the provisions of such a [retraction] law should be, particularly on the subject of punitive damages." The article recounted Juliette Smith's case against the *Buffalo Morning Express* and *Illustrated Express,* where a state appeals court found that recklessness or carelessness was sufficient to support a verdict for punitive damages. Echoing the concerns of the press associations, the article argued that "it is manifestly impossible for publishers to verify all the news they receive, before its publication," and such verification should not be necessary when there is reason to trust it is from "regular and supposedly reliable channels." It concluded, "It would seem to be wise to draw a clear distinction between malicious and inadvertent or unintentional libel, making publishers, in the latter case, liable only for the damages actually shown to have been caused by the erroneous publication."[50] An article in the following issue of the same journal praised the newly passed Pennsylvania retraction statute, which limited plaintiffs in civil libel cases to actual damages. The unnamed author argued that the law would end "speculative libel suits," and that New York "ought to have such a law on its statute books."[51]

The aspirations and reservations of the press and bar associations became manifest in the seventeen retraction statutes passed by state legislatures between 1885 and 1915, and echoed through the legal reasoning of judges considering their validity. Twelve of the seventeen statutes were passed between 1895 and 1905: Indiana and Illinois in 1895, Utah, Wisconsin, Massachusetts, and Pennsylvania in 1897, New Jersey in 1898, Alabama and Washington in 1899, Ohio in 1900, North Carolina in 1901, and Maine in 1903.[52] Only Michigan and Minnesota preceded this push, in 1885 and 1887, respectively.[53] Kentucky and South Dakota were added in 1909 and 1915, respectively.[54] Meanwhile, over the same time period supreme courts in five states ruled on whether the statutes were consistent with state constitutions: in Michigan in 1888,[55] Minnesota in 1889,[56] Kansas and North Carolina in 1904,[57] and Ohio in 1911.[58]

The seventeen statutes differed in a variety of ways, but they all placed explicit limits on the damages a plaintiff could recover when the defendant issued a timely retraction and presented evidence that the falsehood was published accidentally and without malice. Many of the statutes used language that was similar to the statute that the press associations favored, from Minnesota. Four of them were nearly identical to that law. Six of the statutes included the requirement that plaintiffs notify defendants and identify the specific libelous material at least three days before filing a lawsuit. Those were Minnesota, Alabama, Washington, Kansas, North Carolina, and South Dakota.[59]

Thirteen of the seventeen statutes explicitly singled out newspapers for protection. The Michigan, Minnesota, Indiana, Illinois, Utah, Wisconsin, Washington, Kansas, North Carolina, and South Dakota statutes applied to newspapers only;[60] the New Jersey and Kentucky laws applied to newspapers and other publications,[61] and part of the Alabama law applied to newspapers, but the other part applied to all defendants.[62] The Massachusetts, Pennsylvania, Ohio, and Maine statutes did not specify newspapers, publications, or other types of defendants.[63]

Several of the statutes made specific reference to the democratic role of newspapers in covering public proceedings, or in making "public information" available.[64] For example, the Wisconsin law codified a standard common law privilege for reporting defamatory statements uttered in an official proceeding, such as a trial, legislative debate, or political speech.[65] The Pennsylvania standard banned the recovery of any damages in a civil libel suit when the information at issue was "true and proper for public information."[66] Meanwhile, in spite of the strong protections against libel suits involving political or public interest speech, some legislators made sure to include protection from "October surprise" chicanery in elections. Six of the laws did not allow the limitation on damages to apply in suits brought by political candidates when the retraction was made fewer than a specified number of days before an election—usually three days for daily papers, ten days for weekly papers.[67]

In the midst of the lobbying push, ABA president Moorfield Storey synthesized why many members of the bar and bench should resist extending special legal protection to newspapers, but he also offered a reason for those opposed to the laws to be optimistic. In an 1896 address, Storey argued that rivalry among newspapers "leads them . . . to treat as public property what we have been wont to consider matter[s] of essentially private concern." Given the deadline constraints facing competing newspapers, "editors and reporters have no time to sift evidence or to hear both sides." Moreover, "the sensational newspaper sometimes finds its victims resentful, and its proprietors have conceived a prejudice against the common law of libel. Hence in most of the states the attempt has been made to amend it." However, although retraction statutes enable "newspapers to proceed with less care and to reap profit of a scandalous sensation on somewhat easy terms. . . . It is probable . . . that juries and courts may be relied upon to interpret [them] in the interests of public justice."[68] Indeed, the press associations' new influence in legal thinking about protecting their social role collided with legislators and judges that challenged both their claims to that role as well as the premise that their right to press freedom might be favored over an individual's right to protect his or her reputation.

Concerns about "class legislation" arose as the statutes were challenged in court. In 1888 the Michigan Supreme Court struck down that state's retraction statute as violating the state constitution. In *Park v. Free Press Co.*, the court ruled that the law gave "one class of citizens legal exemptions from liability for wrongs not granted to others." It was not necessarily in the classifying itself that the court saw a problem, but rather the outcome stemming from that classification: the treatment of the state's journalists as owing a lesser duty of care for fellow citizens' reputations than other individuals or groups owed.[69] Other courts, however, had a less difficult time with the proposition. In *Allen v. Pioneer Press Co.,* decided the year after *Park,* the Minnesota Supreme Court upheld that state's retraction statute. The *Allen* court concluded that a law could single out a class of persons for different treatment when the distinction was not arbitrary and was based on a public policy reason. Where the Michigan Supreme Court saw the law extending a license for carelessness to the press, the Minnesota Supreme Court saw a rational distinction made with a public policy purpose, specifically:

> In view of the nature of the business in which they are engaged, and the fact that newspapers are the channels to which the public look for general and important news, and that, even in the exercise of the greatest care and vigilance, and actuated by the best of motives, they are liable through

> honest and excusable mistake to publish what may afterwards prove to be false, we cannot say that it is either arbitrary or without reason of public policy to make such provisions as are made by this act for the special protection of newspaper publishers when sued for libel.[70]

Similarly, in 1904 the North Carolina Supreme Court ruled in *Osborn v. Leach* that, insofar as the state's retraction statute extended a reasonable remedy to all newspapers and periodicals, which were particularly prone to libel suits when they made mistakes but could also promptly retract those mistakes, "we do not think it a discrimination forbidden by the Constitution."[71] In Oakley's suit against the *Cincinnati Post,* the Sixth Circuit federal court likened a plaintiff's demanding and receiving a retraction to a person waiving the right to a jury trial. Although it was not noted in the court's opinion, the Ohio statute also did not explicitly single out newspapers for protection, which might have helped it avoid the class legislation problem.[72]

However, a larger problem that the statutes raised, and the issue on which the Michigan, Kansas, North Carolina, and Ohio supreme courts agreed, was that the statutes unconstitutionally infringed individuals' rights to protect their reputations. The opinion of Justice Campbell of the Michigan Supreme Court was clear and forceful enough that he was quoted at length by each subsequent court that overturned a retraction statute between 1888 and 1911, and his opinion was echoed in later law journal articles opposing the statutes.[73] As with the question of "class legislation," Campbell's reasoning arose both from what he saw as a basic denial of rights as well as the consequences of the statute. By limiting recovery in some libel cases to the damages that plaintiffs could show as a loss in property, business, or trade, the statute made compensation for a wrong very difficult for all plaintiffs, and impossible for some:

> A woman who is slandered in her chastity is under this law usually without any redress whatever. A man whose income is from fixed investment or salary or official emolument or business not depending upon his repute could lose no money directly. . . . The statute does not reach cases where a libel has operated to cut off chances of office or employment in the future, or broken up or prevented relationships not capable of an exact money standard, or produced that intangible but fatal influ-

ence which suspicion, helped by ill will, spreads beyond recall or reach by apology or retraction.[74]

In other words, the Michigan retraction statute failed to account for the imprecise but very real harm done by libel, and the right of citizens to recover damages for that harm. "There is no room for holding in a constitutional system that private reputation is any more subject to be removed by statute from full legal protection than life, liberty, or property. It is one of those rights necessary to human society that underlie the whole social scheme of civilization," Campbell wrote.[75] It is worth noting that several retraction statutes passed after the *Park* decision appear to have paid heed to Campbell's concerns by specifically stating that they did not apply to libels of women.[76]

Subsequent state supreme court opinions in Kansas, North Carolina, and Ohio incorporated Campbell's reasoning, holding that the retraction statutes were an unconstitutional infringement of libel plaintiffs' due process rights and exceeded the limits of legislative authority.[77] In *Allen v. Pioneer Press Co.,* on the other hand, the court ruled that a prompt and prominent retraction of libel offered a suitable remedy for a wrong that carried no tangible monetary value. Moreover, the court ruled that the concept of an "adequate remedy" for a wrong "is subject to variation and modification, as the state of society changes . . . hence a wide latitude must, of necessity, be given to the legislature in determining both the form and the measure of the remedy for a wrong."[78]

Time may have proven the *Allen* court right. More retraction statutes eventually passed—thirty-one states have them today[79]—and the courts gradually embraced more press-protective principles in libel law. In the 1930s and 1940s, courts began to recognize a wire service defense more widely and to limit plaintiffs' recovery of large damages for the republication of libelous statements.[80] By 1964, the U.S. Supreme Court unanimously ruled that "the central meaning of the First Amendment" included a right to criticize public officials even if those criticisms included factual errors or defamatory statements.[81]

Journalists and publisher defendants could largely thank the press associations and their influence for laying the groundwork for a more press-friendly libel law. The press associations' success in persuading seventeen state legislatures to adopt retraction statutes at the turn of the twentieth century illustrates a growing influence in the legal and political sphere, and was especially noteworthy given that it lacked a clear policy benefit for the broader public: the statutes directly and almost exclusively protected newspapers, to the detriment of defamed plaintiffs. The consistency in form and function of the retraction statutes modeled by the press associations and adopted by state legislatures also shows the strength of the associations' ability to influence an idea of a report that considered an accidental untruth that was promptly retracted to be more forgivable than a purposeful and malicious one. More broadly, the gradual acceptance of the retraction statutes and wire service and republication defenses demonstrates how gradually changing legal consciousness on the issue of libel affected the law, a breakthrough for the press's argument that connected the business of gathering and disseminating information, and its dependence on mass communication technology in the process, to legal protection for newspapers' social role in the democratic public sphere.

*Minnesota Retraction Statute*
*1887 Minn. Laws 308*
*General Laws of Minnesota for 1887: Chapter 191*
*Be it enacted by the Legislature of the State of Minnesota:*

SECTION 1. Before any suit shall be brought for the publication of a libel in any newspaper in this state, the aggrieved party shall, at least three (3) days before filing or serving a complaint in such suit, serve notice on the publisher or publishers of said newspaper at their principal office of publication, specifying the statements in the said article which he or they allege to be false and defamatory, if it shall appear on the trial of said action, that the said article was published in good faith, that its falsity was due to mistake or misapprehension of the facts and that a full and fair retraction of any statement therein alleged to be erroneous was published in the next regular issue of such newspaper, or within three (3) days after such misapprehension was brought to the knowledge of such publisher or publishers, in as conspicuous as place and type in such newspaper as was the article complained of as libellous, then the plaintiff in such case shall recover only actual damages. *Provided, however,* That the provisions of this act shall not apply to the case of any libel against any candidate for public office in this state, unless the retraction of the charge is made editorially in a conspicuous manner at least three (3) days before the election.

SEC. 2. The words "actual damages" in the foregoing section shall be construed to include all the damages that the plaintiff may show he has suffered in respect to his property, business, trade, profession or occupation, and no other damages whatever.

SEC. 3. This act shall take effect and be in force from and after its passage.

Approved March 2d, 1887.

# *CONCLUSION*

-·-·/---/-·/-·-·/·-··/··-/···/··/---/-·/

The turn of the twentieth century was a period of dynamic change in the relationship between the press and the public in America. As concerns about privacy, reputation, and propriety were rising in polite society, the press was developing competing approaches to serving news to the public that sparked interest and engagement. The debate documented here surrounding an unprecedented string of serial libel lawsuits and an organized effort to reform libel statutes offers a rich view of the nuanced ways the press and the public negotiated the interrelated roles of journalism, technology, and law in a democratic society. As a subject of historical study, the legal debate that played out in courtrooms, meeting halls, and the court of public opinion can be seen as both illustrative and instrumental. That is, it reflected changing and clashing social and legal consciousness related to the role of journalism in that era, but it also influenced the formulation of new ways of thinking about that role that would carry over into the following century. The serial libel cases and the concurrent retraction statute debate tied the press's economically motivated reliance on wire service news disseminated by mass communication technology to an idea of an acceptable journalistic report that would have extended special legal protection to the modern press in order to fulfill its role in serving the public. Only a few judges agreed with this conception of an idea of a report, and the press found only limited overall success in advancing this rationale as a means to ease their burden in libel law.[1] However, as is sometimes the case in law and in history, the minority view gradually gained ground over time, and through the middle of the next century judges and lawmakers became more willing to accept an exception to the republication rule for defamatory wire service content, a limit to multiple lawsuits over the same defamatory publication, and statutory provisions that lowered damage awards where a libelous publication had been retracted. The serial libel suits served as an object lesson in the perils of combining careless sensationalism with industrialized speed and scale but they also helped the press begin to organize and formulate the broader social conception of journalism as a public good along with legal rationales for protections that would develop in the coming decades.

The debate over the serial libel suits and retraction statutes played out alongside other, more heralded and heavily studied questions of late nineteenth-century libel law, such as whether courts should recognize a privilege for false statements made in the context of political criticism.[2] The scholarship exploring the development of these legal standards provides background for the "actual malice" rule adopted in the celebrated *Sullivan* case of 1964, which extended nearly absolute protection for "uninhibited, robust, and wide-open" debate on the performance of public officials.[3] The story told here throws this developing legal history into further relief: demonstrating how commercial concerns played a key role in the press's idea of an acceptable report and the legal consciousness surrounding libel law alongside more traditional concerns about chilling effects and protecting the public's right to know. While publishers' concerns that the serial libel cases could threaten the news wires and stanch the free flow of information were profound, the defenses proposed in courts and the retraction statutes passed by legislatures were also pragmatic, aimed at allowing them to manage the risks posed by continuing to market the news as a product that mixed public service and sensationalism, delivered at maximum speed and scale.

Moreover, the effort to secure retraction statutes shows how the new professional organizations of the press consolidated and wielded influence over policy, even where connections to broader democratic values, the public interest, or the First Amendment were not clear or compelling. This provides an important early look at how the institutional press can operate as a lobbyist in its own interest, which adds to our growing understanding of the ways in which, contrary to conventional wisdom about journalistic neutrality and objectivity, the press is itself a political interest group, acting as strategic litigants, public policy stakeholders, and active influencers of our conception of democratic values and principles.[4]

Technology, in the form of the electric telegraph, was a linchpin in the matrix of law, journalism, and the public sphere in the serial libel cases and retraction statute debates. It was the *sine qua non* of the threat of serial libel that arose at the end of the nineteenth century and was crucial to the concerns that prompted statutory libel law reform. A proper understanding of the role of the telegraph in these episodes acknowledges that journalists linked the power of that technological tool—its speed and efficiency in disseminating information and the news wires' crucial role in the booming business of news publishing—to their articulation of the special democratic duty of the press to disseminate a vast range of information to the public as quickly and as widely as possible. The press's legal arguments articulated the need for wider latitude to accept the possibility that harmful errors might occur in this essential news dissemination process, which was preferable and more democratically acceptable than chilling newspapers' use of the telegraph in favor of protecting the reputation rights of a relative few individuals who were the victims of unfortunate accidents.

In addition to illuminating the specific ways in which the institutional press linked a legal argument about newspapers' social role and professional identity to the commercial imperative of using wire service technology, the story of the serial libel cases and retraction statute debate shows the integral role legal consciousness plays in the broader social process of formulating the idea of an acceptable journalistic report and in negotiating the limits of the concept of press freedom. This contention rests on the idea that both law and journalism are socially constructed and constitutive. In other words, both are created and limited by social institutions and processes that define and delineate their role in democratic society. The cases and debates examined here should serve as historically important examples of how American society constantly uses law and legal consciousness to regulate journalism; confronting problems created by the use of technology, assessing evolving professional standards, and weighing competing and conflicting ideas about precisely how free the press should be.

The discourse about serial libel and retraction statutes rarely included explicit references to the freedoms of speech and press protected by the First Amendment.[5] This does not mean, however, that the episode cannot offer insight into the history of that essential American democratic provision. The press's position that the use of technology in gathering and disseminating information required legal protection and its use of institutional influence to push for statutes recognizing that idea can shed a helpful historical light on an active scholarly debate about the purpose of the First Amendment and its division between "speech" and "the press."[6] Recently, legal scholars have offered competing historical analyses of the meaning and interpretation of the press clause. One side takes a "press-as-technology" approach, concluding through an examination of the rhetoric of the founders and its subsequent interpretation by the courts that the dominant understanding of "freedom of the press" has been as protection for any user of technology in publishing speech, and not as separate protection for the news publishing industry.[7] A "press-as-industry" argument counters that an examination of the broader experience with printing during the founding era shows that the intention was to protect the valuable function that the press of that era served—informing the public and checking government abuses—as a means to ensure a healthy democracy. This side maintains that, over time, as printing, publishing, and distribution technology have overlapped less with that key "watchdog" function, the broader protection for freedom of speech has all but subsumed the more targeted protection of the press's function.[8]

The serial libel cases and the retraction statute debate offer a richer understanding of the place of the press clause in legal consciousness at a pivotal era for the press and the First Amendment. The turn of the twentieth century was a moment when the lived experience of the press in the public sphere was marked by struggle between the core democracy-serving function of a public interest institution and the need to drive revenue through reader interest. On the one hand, judges that refused to extend special libel defenses to newspapers or state legislators or courts that saw libel law reform as unjustly favorable to that industry can be seen as adopting a "press-as-technology" approach and offering no special rights or treatment to the press as an industry. On the other hand, the organizational success of the press started libel law down a path toward special protections in contexts that only pertained to that industry and its special use of technology—a complex electronic network to spread information—making "press-as-industry" protection a part of their legal landscape. The serial libel cases and the press's response support the idea that, if not as a matter of constitutional interpretation, at least as a matter of public policy, treating the press as a unique institution in need of special treatment was part of the lived legal experience. The account provided here of the discourse both inside and outside of traditional legal forums addressing libel law can help us understand how the institutional press clause and an understanding of the press as an industry requiring special legal protection was formulated and openly debated as a concept as well as supported by the institution itself at the turn of the twentieth century.

In recent years, of course, the Internet has enabled many individuals to gather and publish information at a speed and scale formerly only possible through the resources of large news media institutions. This shift has led some to argue that "we're all journalists now" and that special legal status for the institutional press no longer makes sense in a democratic society, if it ever did.[9] The Internet has also complicated legal thinking around libel, privacy, and publicity, and a historical understanding that acknowledges the interrelationship of technology with evolving ideas about reputation and the public sphere could provide much-needed insight to ongoing debates. In 1996, Congress passed the Communications Decency Act, a law intended to limit the availability of pornography online. The U.S. Supreme Court struck down much of the law as an unconstitutional abridgement of free speech in the landmark case *Reno v. American Civil Liberties Union,*[10] but left in place the "good Samaritan provision," Section 230, which limits civil liability of "interactive computer service providers" for content posted by third-party users.[11] The provision was intended to encourage free speech on the Internet without requiring that websites police the actions of millions of users on the threat of being held liable for the users' tortious speech. In the following decade, courts interpreted the law as a strong shield for website owners and operators from libel suits based on the postings of users.

In addition to helping news websites offer freewheeling comment sections, Section 230 has helped massive social media platforms emerge by significantly reducing the considerable burden they would bear if they were expected to closely monitor the speech of their users. One of the most popular social media platforms, Twitter, even prompted legal commentators to coin the term "twibel" as the potential for users to make and endlessly repeat false and harmful statements about each other became apparent. Scholars have generally found that the single publication rule and

Section 230 would strictly limit any single "twibel" plaintiff from launching a massive serial libel suit, let alone getting much compensation at all.[12] Legal scholar David Ardia has observed that Section 230 "upended a set of principles enshrined in common law doctrines that had developed over decades, if not centuries."[13] Critics of the law have argued that it should be curtailed, as it has "fed an untruthful and irresponsible environment for online dialogue" because neither posters nor website operators are required "to substantiate the truth of what they say, or take responsibility for the harm caused by any falsehoods they spread."[14] In 2010, soon-to-be Supreme Court Justice Elena Kagan observed in her nomination hearing that legal standards that benefit publishers, such as Section 230 or even the "actual malice" standard for public officials and public figures derived from the *Sullivan* doctrine, might be ripe for reconsideration in the digital age. "When something goes around the Internet and everybody believes something false about a person, that's a real harm," Kagan said. "And the legal system should not pretend that it's not."[15]

As contemporary journalism contends with the complex and confounding influence of new technology and a heightened state of uncertainty about professional identity, it is important to consider the lessons offered by a similar period of dynamic change just over one hundred years in the past. Given the tendency of legal thought and institutions to respond to and incorporate such changes gradually and unevenly, even as the times seem to demand immediate reaction, it may be another century before the legal significance of present-day upheaval in journalism and mass communication begins to become clear. After all, the serial libel cases did not arise until nearly fifty years after newspapers organized the first wire service, and widespread recognition of the wire service and libel syndicate defenses would not occur for another thirty to fifty years. Now, at the cusp of yet another moment of change at the intersection of journalism, technology, and law, we can expect to see new definitions of "good" news and "bad" news arise amid a debate about the appropriate scale and scope of the journalistic networks in democratic society.

# *NOTES*

-·/---/-/·/···/

## INTRODUCTION

1. The stories are reprinted in Oakley's suits, for example, Butler v. News-Leader Co., 51 S.E. 213, 241 (Va. 1905) and Butler v. Barret & Jordan, 130 F. 944, 946 (C.C.D. Pa. 1904). Oakley used her legal name, Annie Butler, in her lawsuits. The suits and case of misuse of identity are recounted in chapter 5 here and in Shirl Kasper, *Annie Oakley* (Norman: University of Oklahoma Press, 1992), 174–75; Glenda Riley, *The Life and Legacy of Annie Oakley* (Norman: University of Oklahoma Press, 1994), 77; Thomas Julin and D. Patricia Wallace, "Who's that Crack-Shot Trouser Thief?" *Litigation* 28, no. 4 (2002): 49–67, 50; and Louis Stotesbury, "The Famous 'Annie Oakley' Libel Suits," *American Printer* 40, no. 6 (August 1905): 533.

2. See James Carey, "The Communications Revolution and the Professional Communicator," *Sociological Review Monograph*, no. 13 (January 1969): 23–38; Daniel Czitrom, *Media and the American Mind from Morse to McLuhan* (Chapel Hill: University of North Carolina Press, 1982), 3–29; and Richard John, *Network Nation: Inventing American Telecommunications* (Cambridge, MA: Belknap Press of Harvard University Press, 2010).

3. See Lawrence Friedman, *Guarding Life's Dark Secrets: Legal and Social Controls over Reputation, Propriety, and Privacy* (Stanford, CA: Stanford University Press, 2007); and Samantha Barbas, *Laws of Image: Privacy and Publicity in America* (Stanford, CA: Stanford University Press, 2015).

4. See Norman Rosenberg, *Protecting the Best Men: An Interpretive History of the Law of Libel* (Chapel Hill: University of North Carolina Press, 1986), 13–15, 204–6, 125–29.

5. See Friedman, *Guarding Life's Dark Secrets*; Barbas, *Laws of Image*.

6. See Friedman, *Guarding Life's Dark Secrets*; Barbas, *Laws of Image*; Diane Borden, "Beyond Courtroom Victories: An Empirical and Historical Analysis of Women and the Law of Defamation" (PhD diss., University of Washington, 1993).

7. The "wire service defense," a qualified privilege that can block a libel suit against a news organization for defamatory statements when they were received and republished from a reliable wire service, gained judicial recognition in about half of the United States beginning in the 1930s. See Kyu Ho Youm, "The 'Wire Service' Libel Defense," *Journalism*

*Quarterly* 70, no. 3 (1993): 682–91. Primary and secondary sources cite Layne v. Tribune Co., 108 Fla. 177 (1933) as the first time the wire service defense was recognized.

Courts began to recognize a "single publication rule," under which a plaintiff cannot sue the same publisher more than once for the same article and can receive damages only once for a single libelous article regardless of how often it is republished elsewhere, in the 1940s. The single publication rule was recognized in Hartmann v. Time, Inc., 166 F.2d 12 (3d Cir. 1947), cert denied 334 U.S. 838 (1948). In 1952, a Uniform Single Publication Act was drafted by the National Conference of Commissioners on Uniform State Laws in 1952, and appears in *Restatement 2d of Torts* (1977), § 577A. Most states have adopted the rule through legislation or court recognition.

8. *New York Times* v. Sullivan, 376 U.S. 254 (1964).

9. See, e.g., State v. Derry, 20 Mo. App. 552, 557 (1886), Brewer v. Chase, 121 Mich. 526, 576 (1899); Martin L. Newell, *The Law of Defamation, Libel and Slander in Civil and Criminal Cases: As Administered in the Courts of the United States of America* (Chicago: Callaghan, 1890), 350; Thomas Cooley, *A Treatise on The Law of Torts, or, the Wrongs Which Arise Independent of Contract*, 2nd ed. (Chicago: Callaghan, 1888), 259; and John Townshend, *A Treatise on the Wrongs Called Slander and Libel: And on the Remedy by Civil Action for Those Wrongs*, 4th ed. (New York: Baker, Vorhis & Co., 1890).

10. See James Carey, "The Problem of Journalism History," *Journalism History* 1, no. 1 (1973): 3–5, 27; and Robert Gordon, "Critical Legal Histories," *Stanford Law Review* 36 (1984): 120–24.

11. Carey, "The Problem of Journalism History," 27.

12. James Carey, *Communication as Culture* (Boston: Unwin Hyman, 1989), 18.

13. Michael Schudson has argued that Carey's call for a cultural history of reporting is "the most important . . . of all his pleas" but that "it is a matter of great difficulty to figure out just what [changes in the report] portend for 'consciousness'" ("The Problem of Journalism History, 1996," in *James Carey: A Critical Reader,* ed. E. S. Munson and C. A. Warren [Minneapolis: University of Minnesota Press, 1997], 79–85, 80–81). See also Andie Tucher, "Notes on a Cultural History of Reporting," *Cultural Studies* 23, no. 2 (March 2009): 289–98; and Kathy Roberts Forde and Katherine A. Foss, "'The Facts—The Color!—The Facts' The Idea of a Report in American Print Culture, 1885–1910," *Book History* 15 (2012): 123–51.

14. Susan S. Silbey, "After Legal Consciousness," *Annual Review of Law & Social Science* 1 (2005): 323–68. See also Susanna Blumenthal, "Of Mandarins, Legal Consciousness, and the Cultural Turn in US Legal History: Robert W. Gordon. 1984. Critical Legal Histories, Stanford Law Review 36: 57–125," *Law & Social Inquiry* 37 (2012): 167.

15. David Rabban, *Free Speech in Its Forgotten Years* (New York: Cambridge University Press, 1997). See, e.g., Margaret A. Blanchard, "Filling in the Void: Free Speech and the Press in State Courts prior to Gitlow," in *The First Amendment Reconsidered: New Perspectives in the Meaning of Freedom Speech and Press,* ed. Bill F. Chamberlin and

Charlene J. Brown (New York: Longman, 1982); Donna Lee Dickerson, *The Course of Tolerance: Freedom of the Press in Nineteenth-Century America* (Westport, CT: Greenwood Press, 1990); and Timothy Gleason, *The Watchdog Concept: The Press and the Courts in Nineteenth Century America* (Ames: University of Iowa Press, 1990).

16. Gleason, *The Watchdog Concept*; and Dean C. Smith, "The Real Story behind the Nation's First Shield Law: Maryland, 1894–1897," *Communication Law & Policy* 19 (2014): 3–53.

17. See Frederick Schauer, "Towards an Institutional First Amendment," *Minnesota Law Review* 89 (2005): 1256–79; Eugene Volokh, "Freedom for the Press as an Industry, or Freedom for the Press as a Technology? From the Framing to Today," *University of Pennsylvania Law Review*160 (2011): 459–540; Sonja West, "'The Press,' Then & Now," *Ohio State Law Journal* 77 (2016): 49–105, and West, "Awakening the Press Clause," *UCLA Law Review* 58 (2011): 1025–70.

18. Carolyn Marvin, *When Old Technologies Were New: Thinking about Electric Communication in the Late Nineteenth Century* (New York: Oxford University Press, 1988); John, *Network Nation*; and Richard Kielbowicz, "Regulating Timeliness: Technologies, Laws, and the News, 1840–1970," *Journalism and Communication Monographs* 17, no. 1 (2015): 5–83.

19. Jeffery A. Smith, "Moral Guardians and the Origins of the Right to Privacy," *Journalism and Communication Monographs* 10, no. 1 (2008): 63–110.

20. W. Joseph Campbell, *The Year that Defined American Journalism: 1897 and the Clash of Paradigms* (New York: Routledge, 2006).

21. Michael Schudson, *Discovering the News: A Social History of American Newspapers* (New York: Basic Books, 1978); Paul Starr, *The Creation of Mass Media: Political Origins of Modern Communications* (New York: Basic Books, 2005), 153–89; John, *Network Nation*; Gerald Baldasty, *The Commercialization of the News in the Nineteenth Century* (Madison: University of Wisconsin Press, 1992); and Menahem Blondheim, *News over the Wires: The Telegraph and the Flow of Public Information in America, 1844–1897* (Cambridge, MA: Harvard University Press, 1994).

## CHAPTER 1: NEWS IN THE LATE NINETEENTH CENTURY

1. See Daniel Walker Howe, *What Hath God Wrought: The Transformation of America, 1815–1848* (New York: Oxford University Press, 2007), 1–7, 690–98; Lacy K. Ford Jr., "Frontier Democracy: The Turner Thesis Revisited," *Journal of the Early Republic* 13 (1993): 144–63; Patricia Kelly Hall and Steven Ruggles, "'Restless in the Midst of Their Prosperity': New Evidence on the Internal Migration of Americans, 1850–2000," *Journal of American History* 91 (2004): 829–46; and Lawrence M. Friedman, *Guarding Life's Dark Secrets: Legal and Social Controls over Reputation, Propriety, and Privacy* (Stanford, CA: Stanford University Press, 2007), 7, 27–30.

2. James Fenimore Cooper, *The American Democrat* (Cooperstown, NY: H & E Phinney, 1838), 131.

3. Norman L. Rosenberg, *Protecting the Best Men: An Interpretive History of the Law of Libel* (Chapel Hill: University of North Carolina Press, 1986), 137–40. Rosenberg called Cooper's legal crusade "unmatched" until the 1930s and 1940s, when Congressman Martin Sweeney launched a chain of libel suits against the columnist Drew Pearson. This book challenges that characterization.

4. General overviews of the development of the popular press are found in William E. Huntzicker, *The Popular Press, 1833–1865* (Westport, CT: Greenwood Press, 1999); John D. Stevens, *Sensationalism and the New York Press* (New York: Columbia University Press, 1991); Hazel Dicken-Garcia, *Journalistic Standards in Nineteenth-Century America* (Madison: University of Wisconsin Press, 1989); John C. Nerone, "The Mythology of the Penny Press," *Critical Studies in Mass Communication* 4, no. 4 (1987): 376–405; Michael Schudson, *Discovering the News: A Social History of American Newspapers* (New York: Basic Books, 1981); and Alfred M. Lee, *The Daily Newspaper in America: The Evolution of a Social Instrument* (New York: Macmillan, 1937).

5. See Samantha Barbas, *Laws of Image: Privacy and Publicity in America* (Stanford, CA: Stanford University Press, 2015), 26–44; Jeffery Smith, "Moral Guardians and the Origins of the Right to Privacy," *Journalism and Communication Monographs* 10, no. 1 (2008): 64–110; Friedman, *Guarding Life's Dark Secrets*, 4. See also Richard Wightman Fox, *Trials of Intimacy: Love and Loss in the Beecher-Tilton Scandal* (Chicago: University of Chicago Press, 2000); Glenn Wallach, "'A Depraved Taste for Publicity': The Press and Private Life in the Gilded Age," *American Studies* 39, no. 1 (1998); and Rochelle Gurstein, *The Repeal of Reticence: America's Cultural and Legal Struggles over Free Speech, Obscenity, Sexual Liberation, and Modern Art* (New York: Hill and Wang, 1996).

6. Samuel Warren and Louis Brandeis, "The Right to Privacy," *Harvard Law Review* 4 (1890): 193–220, 196. See Benjamin E. Bratman, "Brandeis and Warren's 'The Right to Privacy' and the Birth of the Right to Privacy," *Tennessee Law Review* 69 (Spring 2002): 638–44.

7. Wallach, "A Depraved Taste," 32.

8. W. Joseph Campbell, *The Year That Defined American Journalism: 1897 and the Clash of Paradigms* (New York: Routledge, 2006), 70, 69–117.

9. See Richard Kaplan, *Politics and the American Press: The Rise of Objectivity, 1865–1920* (Cambridge: Cambridge University Press, 2002); and Michael Schudson, "The Objectivity Norm in American Journalism," *Journalism* 2, no. 2 (2001): 149–70. The process of professionalization in journalism has been somewhat contested in the historical literature. Robert Wiebe stated that American journalists joined other groups like teachers, doctors, and lawyers in the push for professionalization in the early 1900s through the adoption of specialized education and attempts to shed negative stereotypes of earlier generations (*The Search for Order: 1877–1920* [New York: Hill and Wang: 1967],

120). Others have argued that the process began earlier. Stephen Banning, for example, argued that the formation of early trade groups with collective aims in the mid-1800s constituted a professional consciousness ("The Professionalization of Journalism: A Nineteenth Century Beginning," *Journalism History* 24, no. 4 [1999]: 157–64). Andie Tucher has argued that the collective sense of purpose expressed by Civil War reporters was indicative of professionalism ("Reporting for Duty: The Bohemian Brigade, the Civil War, and the Social Construction of the Reporter," *Book History* 9 [2006]: 131–57).

10. See, for example, Stephen Banning, "Political or Professional? The Nineteenth Century National Editorial Association," paper delivered at the AEJMC National Conference, Washington, DC, 2013; Banning, "The Professionalization of Journalism"; and Frank E. Fee Jr., "Breaking Bread, Not Bones: Printers' Festivals and Professionalism in Antebellum America," *American Journalism* 30, no. 3 (2013): 308–35. Early descriptions of press associations appear in Frederic Hudson, *Journalism in the United States, from 1690 to 1872* (New York: Harper & Brothers, 1873), 665, and John Weeks Moore, *Moore's Historical, Biographical, and Miscellaneous Gatherings* (Concord, NH: Republican Press Association, 1886), 251–62. On the role of organizations in professionalization, see Arthur Schlesinger, "Biography of a Nation of Joiners," *American Historical Review* 50, no. 16 (1944).

11. Hiley Henry Ward, "Ninety Years of the National Newspaper Association: The Mind and Dynamics of Grassroots Journalism in Shaping America" (Ph.D. dissertation, University of Minnesota, 1977), 49.

12. Dean C. Smith, "The Real Story behind the Nation's First Shield Law: Maryland, 1894–1897," *Communication Law & Policy* 19, no. 3 (2014): 22, citing Harry Wellington Wack, "The International League of Press Clubs," *Overland Monthly* 29 (1897): 631.

13. See Banning, "The Professionalization of Journalism," and Banning, "Not Quite Professional: Bohemian and Elitist Newspaper Clubs in Nineteenth-Century Chicago," *Journalism History* 40, no. 1 (2014): 28–39.

14. See Patrick Lee Plaisance, "A Gang of Pecksniffs Grow Up: The Evolution of Journalism Ethics Discourse in *The Journalist* and *Editor and Publisher*," *Journalism Studies* 6, no. 4 (2005): 479–91; and Mary M. Cronin, "Trade Press Roles in Promoting Journalistic Professionalism, 1884–1917," *Journal of Mass Media Ethics* 8, no. 4 (1993): 227–38.

15. "The Ethics of Modern Journalism," *Newspaperdom,* April 9, 1896, 1.

16. Ibid., 6; see also "Papers and Private Life," *Newspaperdom,* May 28, 1896, 6, regretting newspaper interest in private lives, but also blaming "the public's appetite for that sort of thing."

17. "Muck–rake Journalism," *Newspaperdom,* April 30, 1896, 2.

18. Roosevelt is often credited with associating the term with journalism, but the 1896 essay shows that it was in use at least ten years earlier. The story, and the influential style of investigative journalism the term came to be associated with, is familiar

to students of journalism history. See, for example, Michael Emery, Edwin Emery, and Nancy Roberts, *The Press and America: An Interpretive History of the Mass Media,* 9th ed. (Needham Heights, MA: Allyn & Bacon, 2000), 213; and Bill Kovarik, *Revolutions in Communication: Media History from Gutenberg to the Digital Age* (New York: Continuum, 2011), 76–77.

19. Plaisance, "A Gang of Pecksniffs Grow Up," 483. Plaisance quotes the June 1886 issue of *The Journalist,* which accuses editors of "divesting themselves and their papers of every semblance of dignity; and in the process . . . gaining the hearty contempt of all thinking readers."

20. Lee, *The Daily Newspaper in America,* 70–78, 716–19. In 1830, visiting French political philosopher Alexis de Tocqueville described a typical American as "a very civilized man prepared for a time to face life in the forest, plunging into the wilderness of the New World with his Bible, ax, and newspapers" (*Democracy in America,* ed. J. P. Mayer, trans. George Lawrence [Garden City, NY: Doubleday, 1969 (1835)], 303).

21. On the business of the pre-popular press, see Jeffery A. Smith, *Printers and Press Freedom: The Ideology of Early American Journalism* (New York: Oxford University Press, 1988), 95–107, 202–6; and Frederic Hudson, *Journalism United States from 1690–1872* (New York: J & J Harper, 1873), 141–57. On the changing business model and institutional structure, see Gerald Baldasty, *The Commercialization of News in the Nineteenth Century* (Madison: University of Wisconsin Press, 1992), 82–85; John Nerone and Kevin G. Barnhurst, "US Newspaper Types, the Newsroom, and the Division of Labor, 1750–2000," *Journalism Studies* 4, no. 4 (2003): 438, 443–44.

22. The leading account is Alfred D. Chandler Jr., *The Visible Hand: The Managerial Revolution in American Business* (Cambridge, MA: Harvard University Press, 1977).

23. Baldasty, *The Commercialization of News in the Nineteenth Century,* 82–83.

24. On the history of collaborative news gathering efforts in America, see Richard Schwarzlose, *The Nation's Newsbrokers* (Evanston, IL: Northwestern University Press, 1990); and Victor Rosewater, *History of Cooperative Newsgathering in the United States* (New York: Appleton, 1930).

25. Post Office Act of 1792, 1 Stat. 232 (1792). Exchanges remained an essential part of the news ecosystem even after news wires became common. See Paul Starr, *The Creation of Mass Media: Political Origins of Modern Communications* (New York: Basic Books, 2005), 89–91; Richard John, *Spreading the News: The American Postal System from Franklin to Morse* (Cambridge, MA: Harvard University Press, 1996); Richard Kielbowicz, *News in the Mail: The Press, Post Office, and Public Information, 1700–1860s* (Westport, CT: Greenwood Press, 1972); and Wayne Fuller, *The American Mail: Enlarger of the Common Life* (Chicago: University of Chicago Press, 1972).

26. Oliver Gramling, *AP: The Story of News* (Port Washington, NY: Kennikat Press, 1969), 19–32; Rosewater, *History of Cooperative Newsgathering in the United States,* 57–69.

27. Menahem Blondheim, *News over the Wires: The Telegraph and the Flow of Public*

*Information in America, 1844–1897* (Cambridge, MA: Harvard University Press, 1994), 38. See also Helen MacGill Hughes, *News and the Human Interest Story* (Chicago: University of Chicago Press, 1940), 2–19, 58.

28. See David Mindich, *Just the Facts: How Objectivity Came to Define American Journalism* (New York: New York University Press, 1998).

29. Daniel Czitrom, *Media and the American Mind from Morse to McLuhan* (Chapel Hill: University of North Carolina Press, 1982), 18. See Simon N.D. North, *History and Present Condition of the Newspaper and Periodical Press of the United States* (Washington, DC: Census Office, 1884), 110. North reported, "The influence of the telegraph upon the journalism of the United States has been one of equalization. It has placed the provincial newspaper on a par with the metropolitan journal, so far as the prompt transmission of news—the first and always the chiefest function of journalism—is concerned." See also Richard Kielbowicz, "Regulating Timeliness: Technologies, Laws, and the News, 1840–1970," *Journalism and Communication Monographs* 17, no. 1 (2015).

30. Rosewater, *History of Cooperative Newsgathering in the United States,* 41–43. The practice is still common today.

31. Tom Standage, *The Victorian Internet* (New York: Walker Publishing Co., 1998), 116.

32. "The Manager's Chief Difficulty," *Newspaperdom* 4, no. 15, November 21, 1895, 1.

33. Press Pub. Co. v. McDonald, 63 F. 238, 240 (2d Cir. N.Y. 1894).

34. Ibid.

35. Post Pub. Co. v. Butler, 137 F. 723, 724–25 (6th Cir. Ohio 1905). The first quote is from the editor's testimony, the second from the court's opinion.

36. "United Press Sues a Newspaper," *Newspaperdom,* September 17, 1896, 6.

37. "Accountability of Plate and Ready-Print Concerns," *Newspaperdom,* December 7, 1899, 6.

38. See Emery and Roberts, *The Press and America,* 156–59, 188–89; Starr, *The Creation of Mass Media,* 191–222.

## CHAPTER 2: LIBEL IN THE NINETEENTH CENTURY

1. William B. Odgers, *A Digest of the Law of Libel and Slander,* 5th ed. (London: Stevens, 1881), 161. Odgers attributes the phrase to the 1777 Richard Brinsley Sheridan play, *The School for Scandal.* See also Thomas Cooley, *A Treatise on The Law of Torts, or, the Wrongs Which Arise Independent of Contract,* 2nd ed. (Chicago: Callaghan, 1888), 259; Martin L. Newell, *The Law of Defamation, Libel and Slander in Civil and Criminal Cases: As Administered in the Courts of the United States of America* (Chicago: Callaghan, 1890), 350; and John Townshend, *A Treatise on the Wrongs Called Slander and Libel: And on the Remedy by Civil Action for Those Wrongs,* 4th ed. (New York: Baker, Vorhis & Co., 1890). The common law system of the United States relied on the principle of *stare decisis,* which required courts to help establish legal rules and standards by following the

sound reasoning of previous decisions involving similar facts. Legal treatises like those listed above and discussed in this chapter played an important role in pointing up key cases and using them to articulate and refine those standards amid a growing morass of case law on various subjects. According to legal historian Lyndsay Campbell, treatises "communicated not just procedural rules or digests of cases but frameworks for understanding . . . a body of law." See Campbell, "Libel Treatises and the Transmission of Legal Norms," in *Law Books in Action: Essays on the Anglo-American Legal Treatise,* ed. Angela Fernandez and Markus D. Dubber (Oxford: Hart Publishing, 2012), 169.

2. Frederic Hudson, *Journalism in the United States from 1690 to 1872* (New York: Harper & Bros., 1873), 747. See Norman Rosenberg, *Protecting the Best Men: An Interpretive History of the Law of Libel* (Chapel Hill: University of North Carolina Press, 1986), 197; Timothy Gleason, *The Watchdog Concept: The Press and the Courts in Nineteenth Century America* (Ames: University of Iowa Press, 1990), 66–67; Gleason, "The Libel Climate of the Late Nineteenth Century," *Journalism Quarterly* 70, no. 4 (1993): 893–906, 895. According to John D. Stevens et al., the number of reported criminal libel prosecutions also rose steadily between 1876 and 1906 ("Criminal Libel as Seditious Libel, 1916–65," *Journalism Quarterly* 43 [1966]: 110–13).

3. "The Libel Laws," *Journalist,* March 16, 1895.

4. See Rosenberg, *Protecting the Best Men,* 317n46. The *Central Law Journal* 13 (1881) reported contingency fees were an "all but universal custom of the profession" (381). According to Lawrence Friedman, although "the upper part of the bar looked with beady eyes at this practice, [it] had its merits, [because] it made it possible for the poor man to sue the rich corporation" (*A History of American Law* [New York: Simon and Schuster, 1973], 422–23).

5. John Fabian Witt, *The Accidental Republic: Crippled Workingmen, Destitute Widows, and the Remaking of American Law* (Cambridge, MA: Harvard University Press, 2006), 59–61; John Matzko, "'The Best Men of the Bar': The Founding of the American Bar Association," in *The New High Priests: Lawyers in Post-Civil War America* (Westport, CT: Praeger, 1984), 75–78.

6. According to Gleason, "The case law suggests that newspapers' proclivity toward convicting defendants in criminal actions and inserting editorial comment into news reports generated libel suits" (*The Watchdog Concept,* 66–67).

7. Minutes of ANPA Annual Meetings, 1895, 76; "Boston," *Journalist,* February 2, 1889, 3, and "Boston," *Journalist,* August 29, 1892, 10; "Do Not Publish News of Libel Suits," *Fourth Estate,* July 8, 1894, 4; "Suppressing Libel News," *Newspaperdom,* June 11, 1896, 6.

8. Minutes of ANPA Annual Meetings, 1895, 76.

9. "Union against Shysters" *Fourth Estate,* February 3, 1898, 6.

10. Gleason, "The Libel Climate of the Late Nineteenth Century," 899. Gleason concluded that "few libel plaintiffs won suits, and successful plaintiffs were awarded a

small portion of the requested damage awards. The trade journals reported 143 cases in which damages requested and damages won could be determined. Only fifteen awards of $10,000 or more were reported. The highest award reported was $45,000." Although the trade press is unreliable as a conclusive source of information on libel law, it seems likely that large verdicts, at least, would have drawn coverage.

11. "Vindicator Vindicated," *Newspaperdom,* March 18, 1897, 4.

12. Untitled Editorial, *Journalist,* August 4, 1892, 8; and Gleason, "The Libel Climate of the Late Nineteenth Century," 902, 905–6. According to Gleason, the *New York World* typically paid attorneys annual retainers of $10,000 between 1885 and 1891.

13. "No Frivolous Libel Suits," *Philadelphia Times,* February 9, 1888, quoted in Samuel Merrill, *Newspaper Libel: A Handbook for the Press* (Boston: Ticknor, 1888), 31–32.

14. Minutes of ANPA Annual Meetings, 1895, 79.

15. Patrick File, "'Watchdog' Journalists and 'Shyster' Lawyers: Analyzing Legal Reform Discourse in the Journalistic Trade Press, 1895–1899," *American Journalism* 35, no. 3 (2018), copyright © Taylor & Francis, LLC.

16. "Note and Comment," *Fourth Estate,* March 25, 1897, 6.

17. "Current Comment," *Newspaperdom,* September 17, 1896, 6.

18. "Wisconsin Libel Law," *Newspaperdom,* March 19, 1896, 1; "Palmer Loses," *Fourth Estate,* March 18, 1897, 2; "Libel Laws and Libel Litigations," *Fourth Estate,* February 25, 1897, 11; see also "Libels Against Newsdealers," *Journalist,* March 22, 1884.

19. "Note and Comment," *Fourth Estate,* March 24, 1898, 4.

20. Thomas Haskell, *The Emergence of Professional Social Science* (Urbana: University of Illinois Press, 1977), 40.

21. Witt, *The Accidental Republic,* 44. See also Barbara Welke, *Recasting American Liberty: Gender, Race, Law, and the Railroad Revolution, 1865–1920* (Cambridge: Cambridge University Press, 2001).

22. Oliver Wendell Holmes Jr., *The Common Law* (Boston: Little, Brown, 1881), 63–103, 115–29. See Morton J. Horwitz, *The Transformation of American Law, 1780–1860* (Cambridge, MA: Harvard University Press, 1977), 10–11, 54–65; and Witt, *The Accidental Republic,* 1–21, 43–70.

23. Holmes, *The Common Law,* 96. See Horwitz, *The Transformation of American Law,* 123–24; and Witt, *The Accidental Republic,* 46–49.

24. David Rabban, *Free Speech in Its Forgotten Years* (New York: Cambridge University Press, 1997), 132; Leonard Levy, *Emergence of a Free Press* (New York: Oxford University Press, 1985), 11–13. "Every freeman has an undoubted right to lay what sentiments he pleases before the public," Blackstone declared in *Commentaries on the Laws of England,* "but if he publishes what is improper, mischievous, or illegal, he must take the consequences of his own temerity" (Sir William Blackstone, *Commentaries on the Laws of England,* 4 vols., ed. William Carey Jones [London, 1765–69; reprint, San Francisco: Bancroft-Whitney, 1916], book 4, chap. 11, 152). According to Leonard Levy, Blackstone was "the oracle of the common law in the minds of the American Framers," and his

formulation of the limits of freedom of the press "gripped American thinking" on the subject (*Emergence of a Free Press,* 12, 247). According to Rosenberg, however, a closer look at "the broader legal culture" shows that the Blackstone formulation was pervasive, but not as much as Levy maintains: "During the last quarter of the eighteenth century, numerous Americans flatly rejected the Blackstonian premises that freedom of the press meant merely the absence of prepublication restraints and that any criticism of government and public officials carried criminal liability" (*Protecting the Best Men,* 53–54). See also Jeffery Smith, *Printers and Press Freedom: The Ideology of Early American Journalism* (New York: Oxford University Press, 1988), 62–63.

25. Rabban, *Free Speech in Its Forgotten Years,* 2, 17, 38, 72, 118–19, 132–46.

26. Rosenberg, *Protecting the Best Men,* 125–29; Rabban, *Free Speech in Its Forgotten Years,* 155.

27. The minority view, eventually adopted by the U.S. Supreme Court in *Sullivan,* was that some false speech could be protected when it concerned public officials or issues of public concern. See Clifton Lawhorne, *Defamation and Public Officials: The Evolving Law of Libel* (Carbondale: Southern Illinois University Press, 1971), 122–26; and W. Wat Hopkins, *Actual Malice: Twenty-Five Years after Times v. Sullivan* (New York: Praeger, 1989), 50–52.

28. Rosenberg, *Protecting the Best Men,* 110–11; Levy, *Emergence of a Free Press,* 338–40; Rabban, *Free Speech in Its Forgotten Years,* 202–3.

29. Rosenberg, *Protecting the Best Men,* 115; Levy, *Emergence of a Free Press,* 340.

30. Cooley, *A Treatise on the Law of Torts,* 93, 830.

31. Cooley, *Constitutional Limitations* (1868), 438.

32. See Lawhorne, *Defamation and Public Officials,* 87–110. Lawhorne found that twenty-five of the twenty-eight states that had appellate decisions on political libel granted some privilege for libelous political criticism between the Civil War and 1900.

33. Cooley, *Constitutional Limitations* (1868), 452–56.

34. Miner v. Post & Tribune Co., 13 N.W. 773, at 776 (Mich. 1882).

35. MacLean v. Scripps, 17 N.W. 815, at 818 (1884).

36. Compare Cooley, *Constitutional Limitations* (1868), 454, with Cooley, *Constitutional Limitations,* 5th ed. (Boston: Little, Brown, 1883), 563. See also Norman Rosenberg, "Thomas M. Cooley, Liberal Jurisprudence, and the Law of Libel, 1868–1884," *University of Puget Sound Law Review* 4 (1980): 49.

37. Cooley, *Constitutional Limitations* (1883), 562. See *New York Times v. Sullivan* 376 U.S. 254 at 270 (1964), affirming "a profound national commitment to the principle that debate on public issues should be uninhibited, robust, and wide-open, and that it may well include vehement, caustic, and sometimes unpleasantly sharp attacks on government and public officials," which has become a baseline for the consideration of political libel cases. The *Sullivan* doctrine extends a qualified privilege to publishers discussing public persons or issues. In order to recover damages in a libel

suit, public officials and public figures must show "actual malice": that a publisher of a defamatory statement knew the statement was false and published it anyway or recklessly failed to verify the statement's truth. The Court extended the *Sullivan* rule to public figures in *Curtis Publishing Co. v. Butts,* 388 U.S. 130 (1967). In *Gertz v. Robert Welch, Inc.,* 418 U.S. 323 (1974) the Court identified three classes of potential public figures: (1) those deemed public figures for all purposes, (2) those who thrust themselves to the forefront of a particular controversy and hence become public figures in relation to that issue, and (3) those who become public figures through no purposeful action of their own. See Richard Digby-Junger, "News in Which the Public May Take an Interest: A Nineteenth Century Precedent for *New York Times v. Sullivan,*" *American Journalism* 12, no. 1 (1995): 22–39, for a discussion of the analytical links between Cooley's views on libel and freedom of the press and the reasoning of the *Sullivan* decision.

38. See Horwitz, *The Transformation of American Law,* 109–43; 295n6. See, e.g., Felix Frankfurter, *Mr. Justice Holmes and the Constitution: A Review of His Twenty-Five Years on the Supreme Court* (Cambridge, MA: Dunster House Bookshop, 1927); and Francis Biddle, *Justice Holmes, Natural Law, and the Supreme Court* (New York: Macmillan Company, 1961).

39. Holmes, *The Common Law,* 35–36, 95–96, 110.

40. Ibid., 110; Holmes, "Privilege, Malice, Intent," *Harvard Law Review* 8 (April 1894): 9. For a discussion of the evolution of Holmes's reasoning, see Horwitz, *The Transformation of American Law,* 127–42.

41. Burt v. Advertiser Newspaper Co., 28 N.E. 1, at 4 (1891). The rationale bears a notable resemblance to that of the majority opinion of the U.S. Supreme Court in Milkovich v. Lorain Journal Co. 497 U.S. 1 (1990), in which the court ruled that the First Amendment does not require an absolute privilege for statements of opinion, and that such statements could expose publishers to liability when "sufficiently factual to be susceptible of being proved true or false."

42. Burt v. Advertiser Newspaper Co., 28 N.E. 1, at 5 (1891). Holmes cites Watson v. Moore, 56 Mass. 133, at 140 (1848); Parkhurst v. Ketchum, 88 Mass. 406 (1863); Clark v. Brown, 116 Mass. 504, at 507 (1875) for this statement.

43. Peck v. Tribune Co., 214 U.S. 185, at 188 (1909).

44. Peck v. Tribune Co., 154 F. 330 (7th Cir. 1907).

45. Peck v. Tribune Co., 214 U.S. 185, 189–190 (1909) (internal citations omitted).

46. See Rosenberg, *Protecting the Best Men,* 133. See, e.g., John Townshend, *A Treatise on the Wrongs Called Slander and Libel: And on the Remedy by Civil Action for Those Wrongs,* 4th ed. (New York: Baker, Vorhis & Co., 1890), 104. "The proprietor of a newspaper is responsible for all that appears in its columns, although the publication may have been made without his knowledge, in his absence, or contrary to his orders. His liability is not on the ground of his being the publisher, nor of being

presumed to be the publisher, but because he is responsible for the acts of the actual publisher."

47. See Union Associated Press v. Press Pub. Co., 54 N.Y.S. 183 (N.Y. Sup. Ct. 1898) and Union Associated Press v. Heath, 63 N.Y.S. 96 (N.Y. App. Div. 1900).

48. "The Law of Libel," *Fourth Estate,* January 19, 1899, 8.

49. Newell, *The Law of Defamation, Libel and Slander in Civil and Criminal Cases,* 842–43; and Theodore Sedgwick, *A Treatise on the Measure of Damages, or, An Inquiry into the Principles Which Govern the Amount of Compensation Recovered in Suits at Law,* 8th ed. (New York: Baker, Voorhis, 1891), vol. 1, 502.

50. Newell, *The Law of Defamation, Libel and Slander in Civil and Criminal Cases,* 785.

51. Townshend, *A Treatise on the Wrongs Called Slander and Libel,* 271, 652. See Taylor v. Hearst, 107 Cal. 262, at 271 (Cal. 1895), trial court incorrectly refused to instruct the jury that "you may consider the injury to the plaintiff's feelings" in calculating damages; Butler v. Every Evening Printing Co., 140 F. 934, at 935 (C.C.D. Del. 1905), "The plaintiff sought to recover damages for the injury done to her reputation as well as to her feelings; and it was the effect which the article was calculated to have upon the minds of the mass of its readers, and not any actual intention on the part of the defendant to defame the plaintiff, that was material in the consideration of the injury to reputation. This conclusion is supported by abundant authority." In 1910, the Michigan Supreme Court ruled that "actual damages may be increased by reason of the malice of the defendant, because plaintiff's injury to feelings is greater when he suffers from a wrong wantonly inflicted" (Schattler v. Daily Herald Co., 162 Mich. 115, at 128–29 [Mich. 1910]).

52. Merrill, *Newspaper Libel,* 250.

53. Holmes, *The Common Law,* 126.

54. Merrill, *Newspaper Libel,* 274–75.

55. Townshend, *A Treatise on the Wrongs Called Slander and Libel,* 524–25. See also William Eggleston, *Eggleston on Damages: A Treatise on the Law of Damages* (Terre Haute, IN: Hebb & Goodwin, 1880), 9–10, 633.

56. Spring Co. v. Edgar, 99 U.S. 645 (1878).

57. "The Law of Libel," *Fourth Estate,* January 19, 1899, 8.

58. See Townshend, *A Treatise on the Wrongs Called Slander and Libel,* 117, 133–34; and Newell, *The Law of Defamation, Libel and Slander,* 882–909.

59. See *New York Times v. Sullivan* 376 U.S. 254, at 280 (1964). Justice William Brennan, author of the *Sullivan* decision, later expressed regret at choosing the term "malice" because he thought it confused jurors. See Seth Stern and Stephen Wermiel, *Justice Brennan: Liberal Champion* (New York: Houghton Mifflin Harcourt, 2010), 227.

60. Sedgwick, *A Treatise on the Measure of Damages,* vol. 1, 540.

61. Dole v. Lyon, 10 Johns. 447 (N.Y. Sup. Ct. 1813). See Newell, *The Law of Defamation,* xlvi, 352–53, 356, 656; Townshend, *A Treatise on the Wrongs Called Slander and Libel,* lxvi, 305, 306, 651.

62. Dole v. Lyon, 10 Johns. 447, at 450 (N.Y. Sup. Ct. 1813).

63. Hewitt v. Pioneer-Press Co., 23 Minn. 178, at 180 (Minn. Sup. Ct. 1876). The court cited an 1829 English case, Saunders v. Mills, 6 Bing. 213 (1829).

64. Edwards v. Kansas City Times Co., 32 F. 813, at 819–820 (C.C.W.D. Mo. 1887).

65. Newell, *The Law of Defamation, Libel and Slander,* 893; "Evidence of previous publication by others is inadmissible in mitigation of damages. The fact that others besides the defendant have defamed the plaintiff is a wholly irrelevant matter" (Townshend, *A Treatise on the Wrongs Called Slander and Libel,* 304–5).

66. *Atkinson v. Detroit Free Press,* 46 Mich. 341, 353 (1881).

67. See Newell, *The Law of Defamation,* 253; Peck v. Tribune Co., 214 U.S. 185, 189 (1909).

68. Dole v. Lyon, 10 Johns. 447 (N.Y. Sup. Ct. 1813).

## CHAPTER 3: THE SMITH AND RUTHERFORD CASES

1. Smith v. Sun Printing & Pub. Ass'n, 55 F. 240, at 244 (2d Cir. 1893).

2. Ibid.; Smith v. Matthews, 46 N.E. 164, at 164 (N.Y. 1897).

3. See Smith v. Sun Printing & Pub. Ass'n, 55 F. 240, at 243 (2d Cir.1893) for the version of the story that appeared in the *New York Evening Sun* on June 14, 1890.

4. Smith v. Chicago Herald; see *Chicago Legal News* 26, no. 40 (June 2, 1894): 317–18, for the full opinion of the Circuit Court of Cook County. The opinion is also republished in *Albany Law Journal* 50 (July 7, 1894): 23.

5. The term "libel syndicate defense" is the author's, using the *Fourth Estate*'s 1898 term "libel syndicate" describing the Tyndale Palmer's suits. See "The Past Year," *Fourth Estate,* January 6, 1898.

6. Martin L. Newell, *The Law of Defamation, Libel and Slander in Civil and Criminal Cases: As Administered in the Courts of the United States of America* (Chicago: Callaghan, 1890), 152, 152–66. Newell noted that, in Massachusetts, the doctrine also extended to accusing a woman of being drunk.

7. Smith v. Matthews, 46 N.E. 164 at 165 (N.Y. 1897).

8. Of the three case studies here, the Smith and Rutherford cases yielded the least clarity on how many lawsuits were actually filed. The account here is drawn entirely from the appellate record in four cases: Morning Journal Ass'n v. Rutherford, 51 F. 513 (2d Cir. 1892); Smith v. Sun Printing & Pub. Ass'n, 55 F. 240 (2d Cir. 1893); Smith v. Matthews, 46 N.E. 164 (N.Y. 1897); and Smith v. Chicago Herald, see *Chicago Legal News* 26, no. 40 (June 2, 1894): 317–18.

9. See Smith v. Sun Printing & Pub. Ass'n, 55 F. 240, at 246 (2d Cir. 1893); and Smith v. Chicago Herald, *Chicago Legal News* 26, no. 40 (June 2, 1894): 317.

10. Morning Journal Ass'n v. Rutherford, 51 F. 513, at 515 (2d Cir. 1892); the opinion cited Edwards v. Kansas City Times Co., 32 F. 813 (C.C.W.D. Mo. 1887), the case in which

Judge Brewer instructed a jury that it should consider the accidental republication of libel by a newspaper to be a factor in deciding whether to award punitive damages.

11. Smith v. Chicago Herald, *Chicago Legal News* 26, no. 40 (June 2, 1894): 317.

12. 55 F. 240, at 246 (2d Cir. 1893).

13. 46 N.E. 164 (N.Y. 1897).

14. Smith v. Sun Printing & Pub. Ass'n, 55 F. 240, at 245–46 (2d Cir. 1893).

15. Smith v. Sun Pub. Co., 50 F. 399, at 401 (C.C.D.N.Y. 1892), citing Gibson v. Cincinnati Enquirer, 10 F. Cas. 311 (C.C.S.D. Ohio 1877); John Townshend, *A Treatise on the Wrongs Called Slander and Libel: And on the Remedy by Civil Action for Those Wrongs*, 4th ed. (New York: Baker, Vorhis & Co., 1890), §293; William B. Odgers, *A Digest of the Law of Libel and Slander*, 5th ed. (London: Stevens, 1881), 291.

16. Smith v. Matthews, 6 Misc. 162, at 164 (N.Y. Super. Ct. 1893): "Punitive damages may be awarded not alone where the publication is made in bad faith, and in fact malicious, but where it is recklessly, carelessly or wantonly made." See also Morning Journal Ass'n v. Rutherford, 51 F. 513, at 515 (2d Cir. 1892); Smith v. Sun Pub. Co., 50 F. 399, at 401 (C.C.D.N.Y. 1892); and Smith v. Matthews, 46 N.E. 164, at 165 (N.Y. 1897).

17. Smith v. Sun Pub. Co., 50 F. 399, at 402 (C.C.D.N.Y. 1892).

18. Smith v. Matthews, 46 N.E. 164, at 166 (N.Y. 1897).

19. Morning Journal Ass'n v. Rutherford, 51 F. 513, at 515 (2d Cir. N.Y. 1892).

20. Smith v. Sun Printing & Pub. Ass'n, 55 F. 240, at 246 (2d Cir. N.Y. 1893).

21. Morning Journal Ass'n v. Rutherford, 51 F. 513, at 516 (2d Cir. N.Y. 1892).

22. Smith v. Matthews, 46 N.E. 164, at 166 (N.Y. 1897).

23. See Morton J. Horwitz, *The Transformation of American Law, 1780–1860* (Cambridge, MA: Harvard University Press, 1977), 14–15, 39–43. The doctrine was contested by, among others, Oliver Wendell Holmes Jr. for its refusal to acknowledge a more articulated theory of liability. See Holmes, "Agency" (pts. 1 and 2), *Harvard Law Review* 4, 345, and vol. 5, 1 (1891).

24. Smith v. Matthews, 6 Misc. 162, at 164 (N.Y. Super. Ct. 1893).

25. Dunne would later serve as mayor of Chicago from 1905 to 1907 and governor of Illinois from 1913 to 1917. See Richard Allen Morton, *Justice and Humanity: Edward F. Dunne, Illinois Progressive* (Carbondale: Southern Illinois University Press, 1997).

26. Smith v. Chicago Herald, *Chicago Legal News* 26, no. 40 (June 2, 1894): 317–18.

27. Ibid., 317.

28. Ibid., 317.

29. See John Fabian Witt, *The Accidental Republic: Crippled Workingmen, Destitute Widows, and the Remaking of American Law* (Cambridge, MA: Harvard University Press, 2006), 50–51.

30. Smith v. Chicago Herald, *Chicago Legal News* 26, no. 40 (June 2, 1894): 317. "In cases of physical injuries caused by the negligence of others the injured person is required by law to lessen and reduce the injury so far as it lays within his power, by

medical and surgical attention and personal care and caution. Even in cases of breach of contract the party not in fault is by law held to do all that lie reasonably can to lessen the amount of loss," Dunne wrote.

31. Smith v. Chicago Herald, *Chicago Legal News* 26, no. 40 (June 2, 1894): 317.

32. Ibid. None of the Illinois cases listed involved damages more than $7,000, and most were $3,000 or less. In Indiana, damages were reduced from $8,000 to $2,000 in Curran v. Bridwell, 21 N. E. Rep. 664, in a case "in which an unmarried female was charged with being a prostitute." In Holmes v. Jones, 3 N. Y. S. 156 (N.Y. 1888), "it was held that the verdict for $5,000, for charging a man with blackmailing, shows prejudice, and was excessive." Dunne noted that the highest damage award for libel known at that time was $20,000 in Maclean v. Scripps, 52 Mich. 214 (Mich. 1883). "In that case, however, the question of excessive damages was not raised in the Supreme Court."

33. Smith v. Chicago Herald, *Chicago Legal News* 26, no. 40, June 2, 1894, 317–18.

34. Rutherford v. Morning Journal Ass'n, 47 F. 487, at 488 (C.C.D.N.Y. 1891). See also Smith v. Sun Pub. Co., 50 F. 399 (C.C.D.N.Y. 1892).

35. See Townshend, *A Treatise on the Wrongs Called Slander and Libel,* 524–25: "A case must be very gross, and the damages enormous, to justify ordering a new trial on a question of damages." See also William Eggleston, *Eggleston on Damages: A Treatise on the Law of Damages* (Terre Haute: Hebb & Goodwin, 1880), 9–10, 633.

36. *Newspaperdom,* July 1894, 17.

37. Morning Journal Ass'n v. Rutherford, 51 F. 513, at 516 (2d Cir. N.Y. 1892).

38. Smith v. Chicago Herald, *Chicago Legal News* 26, no. 40 (June 2, 1894): 317.

## CHAPTER 4: THE PALMER CASES

1. See "A Big Theft Discovered," *Pittsburgh Dispatch,* October 2, 1892; "Theft of More than Four Hundred Thousand Dollars," *St. Paul Daily Globe,* October 3, 1892; "Palmer a Youngstown Man," *Pittsburgh Dispatch,* October 3, 1892.

2. "The Past Year," *Fourth Estate,* January 6, 1898.

3. Palmer v. United Press, 67 A.D. 64, at 66 (N.Y. App. Div. 1901), provides the best explanation of how the story reached the United Press wires, although the case leaves aside plenty of questions about the story's origin. See also Palmer v. Matthews, 29 A.D. 149, at 151 (N.Y. App. Div. 1898); "Sued for One Hundred Thousand Dollars Damages," *Winona* (Minnesota) *Daily Republican,* October 6, 1894, 2; and "That Suit for Libel," *Jackson* (Michigan) *Citizen Patriot,* December 13, 1895, 6. It is notable that Palmer sued United Press, the wire service that syndicated the story and a defendant that would be least able to assert a wire service defense. The suit was stymied by the fact that the company went out of business in 1897, leading to procedural and evidentiary problems. The legal issue in the 1901 opinion cited above, for example, was how to proceed in the discovery process—Palmer demanded access to files that the UP claimed no longer existed.

4. "Tireless in Litigation," *Fourth Estate,* November 3, 1898, 4; "Sued for One Hundred Thousand Dollars Damages," *Winona* (Minnesota) *Daily Republican,* October 6, 1894, 2.

5. "A Libel Suit That Fizzled," *Newspaperdom,* April 1894, 477; "Tyndale Palmer Wins One Suit," *Chicago Daily Tribune,* February 2, 1895, 7.

6. U.S. Passport Application, Tyndale Palmer, November 15, 1889.

7 *The History of Washington County, Iowa, Containing a History of the County, Its Cities, Towns &c,* (Des Moines: Union Historical Company, 1880), 431.

8. "Summer Amusements," *Minneapolis Tribune,* May 31, 1885, 3. See also "The City," *Minneapolis Tribune,* June 17, 1885, 5. "Very Nervy: A Gigantic Steal of Nearly Half a Million Dollars," *Maysville* (Kentucky) *Daily Public Ledger,* October 3, 1892, 3.

9. The record of the Palmer and de Freitas cases compiled for this book was drawn, in part, from newspaper and trade press coverage of the lawsuits. As discussed above, it may be incomplete, but it is considered sufficient for the purposes of the broad legal historical discussion here. De Freitas's tandem suits included those against the *Rome* (New York) *Sentinel; St. Louis Post-Dispatch; Utica* (New York) *Observer; Milford* (Massachusetts) *Journal; Lockport* (New York) *Journal; St. Paul Pioneer Press;* and *Winona* (Minnesota) *Daily Republican.* A list of the suits, their disposition (if known), and sources is provided in Table 1.

10. Palmer v. Chicago Herald Co., Same v. Chicago Evening Post Co., 70 F. 886 (C.C.D.N.Y. 1895).

11. See "Those Tyndale Palmer Libel Suits," *Fourth Estate,* July 22, 1897, 1. This article was an incomplete but invaluable resource because it included a table listing the forty-seven known cases and their resolution up to July 1897. Given the challenges associated with nineteenth-century trial court research, it is as fortuitous a primary source as one could hope for, despite the obvious potential for bias in favor of the press. Palmer's approximate average damage claim across the suits collected here was just over $46,000.

12. "Sued for One Hundred Thousand Dollars Damages," *Winona* (Minnesota) *Daily Republican,* October 6, 1894.

13. Palmer v. Matthews, 29 A.D. 149, at 156 (N.Y. App. Div. 1898). Palmer's attorney objected because he argued, successfully in the end, that the total number suits he filed for the same alleged libel was immaterial to the *Illustrated Express'* defense.

14. Editorial, *Fourth Estate,* November 24, 1898, 3.

15. "Those Tyndale Palmer Libel Suits," *Fourth Estate,* July 22, 1897, 1. Palmer v. New York News Pub. Co., 52 N.E. 1125 (N.Y. 1899).

16. "Telegraphic Brevities," *New York Times,* November 13, 1896, 2.

17. "Those Tyndale Palmer Libel Suits," *Fourth Estate,* July 22, 1897, 1.

18. Ibid.

19. Ibid.

20. The research for this book included several full text newspaper databases for keywords related to the cases, including Proquest's America's Historical Newspapers,

The Library of Congress' Chronicling America: Historic American Newspapers, Gale/Infotrac's Nineteenth Century U.S. Newspapers, and Fold3/Ebscohost's Footnote. Approximately forty newspaper articles were collected that mentioned Palmer, de Freitas and their suits, but few of those went beyond basic reportage.

21. "Sued for One Hundred Thousand Dollars Damages," *Winona* (Minnesota) *Daily Republican,* October 6, 1894; the suit was dismissed when neither the plaintiffs nor their attorney showed for a preliminary hearing, and the suit never went to a jury; see "Exit Tyndale Palmer," *Winona* (Minnesota) *Daily Republican,* March 5, 1895.

22. The *Youngstown News* editorial was reprinted in *Newspaperdom.* See "It Depreciates All News," *Newspaperdom,* October 17, 1895, 8.

23. "That Suit for Libel," *Jackson* (Michigan) *Citizen Patriot,* December 13, 1895.

24. See Timothy Gleason, *The Watchdog Concept: The Press and the Courts in Nineteenth Century America* (Ames: University of Iowa Press, 1990), 81–85; Brett Butler Cain, "Contempt by Publication in Nineteenth Century America" (Ph.D. dissertation, University of Alabama, 2007); Walter Nelles and Carol Weiss King, "Contempt by Publication in the United States: To the Federal Contempt Statute," *Columbia Law Review* 28 (1928): 401–31.

25. Such a lacuna of trial coverage has the potential for a far-reaching negative impact on the study of nineteenth-century libel below the appellate level, where newspapers often offer the only source of information where other records cannot be located.

26. See "Do Not Publish News of Libel Suits," *Fourth Estate,* July 8, 1897, 1.

27. "A Libel Suit that Fizzled," *Newspaperdom* 4 (April 1894): 477, reporting on an 1894 Palmer case against the *Alton* (Illinois) *Sentinel-Democrat.*

28. "Tyndale Palmer's Suits," *Fourth Estate,* March 18, 1897, 6.

29. Palmer v. New York News Pub. Co., 52 N.E. 1125 (N.Y. 1899). The *Fourth Estate* also cited a suit Palmer had filed against the *Youngstown Vindicator,* which was dismissed. According to its own reporting in the very same March 18, 1897, issue, however, that suit was not in response to the October 1892 article accusing him of theft but in response to a different article, "written by a friend of Palmer's and . . . thought to be a defence [*sic*] and vindication of him." See "Palmer Loses," *Fourth Estate,* March 18, 1897, 2; see also "Dismissed without Trial," *Cleveland Plain Dealer,* March 9, 1897, and "Vindicator Vindicated," *Newspaperdom,* March 18, 1897, 4. Neither the *Fourth Estate* article nor others reporting the dismissal of the suit explain the court's rationale, and the court itself might not have issued a written opinion. Moreover, astute followers of the Palmer libel suits would have known that a Youngstown jury awarded Palmer $1,350 in his suit against that city's *Telegram* just few months earlier. Had the *Vindicator*'s case reached a jury, its publisher might have had reason to be concerned.

30. "Those Tyndale Palmer Libel Suits," *Fourth Estate,* July 22 1897, 1.

31. "Tyndale Palmer's Suits," *Fourth Estate,* March 18, 1897, 6.

32. "Those Tyndale Palmer Libel Suits," *Fourth Estate,* July 22, 1897, 1.

33. See Smith v. Matthews, 46 N.E. 164 (N.Y. 1897) and Palmer v. Matthews, 162 N.Y. 100 (N.Y. 1900).

34. Palmer v. New York News Pub. Co., 31 A.D. 210, at 216 (N.Y. App. Div. 1898).

35. Palmer v. The Leader Publishing Company 7 Pa. Super. 594 at 597 (Super. Ct. Penn. 1898).

36. In all, this study examined twelve total appeals court rulings in the Palmer cases, ten of which Palmer won on various procedural and evidential issues, some not related to the wire service or libel syndicate defenses or challenging a damage amount. For example, Palmer's three appeals in his case against the *Utica Observer* dealt with whether the testimony of another Auer employee should be allowed or ruled hearsay. See Palmer v. E. P. Bailey & Co., 12 A.D. 6 (Sup. Ct. N.Y. App. Div. 1896); Palmer v. E. P. Bailey & Co., 21 A.D. 630 (N.Y. App. Div. 1897); and Palmer v. E. P. Bailey & Co., 33 A.D. 642 (N.Y. App. Div. 1898). Palmer v. Mahin, 120 F. 737 (8th Cir. Iowa 1903) was related to his serial libel suits, and involved a publisher's claims that Palmer was a blackmailer and extortionist. There the court ruled that the statements were libelous per se and "the victim is as clearly entitled to full compensation for a wrong inflicted with a laudable motive, or through mistake or inadvertence, as from one perpetrated with a diabolical purpose or intent."

37. Palmer v. The Leader Publishing Company 7 Pa. Super. 594 (Super. Ct. Penn. 1898); and Palmer v. Matthews, 162 N.Y. 100 (N.Y. 1900).

38. See Palmer v. E. P. Bailey & Co., 12 A.D. 6 (Sup. Ct. N.Y. App. Div. 1896); Palmer v. E. P. Bailey & Co., 21 A.D. 630 (N.Y. App. Div. 1897); and Palmer v. E. P. Bailey & Co., 33 A.D. 642 (N.Y. App. Div. 1898).

39. Palmer v. The Leader Publishing Company 7 Pa. Super. 594 (Super. Ct. Penn. 1898).

40. Ibid., 597.

41. Palmer v. New York News Pub. Co., 31 A.D. 210 (N.Y. App. Div. 1898).

42. Palmer v. Matthews, 29 A.D. 149, at 155 (N.Y. App. Div. 1898) (Hardin, J. and Follett, J., dissenting).

43. Palmer v. New York News Pub. Co., 31 A.D. 210, at 213—214 (N.Y. App. Div. 1898).

44. The story that alleged that Smith and Rutherford had eloped together was published in the New York papers around the second week of June 1890. See Smith v. Sun Printing & Pub. Asso., 55 F. 240, at 243 (2d Cir. N.Y. 1893).

45. Palmer v. New York News Pub. Co., 31 A.D. 210, at 212 (N.Y. App. Div. 1898), citing Bennett v. Salisbury, 78 F. 769 (2d Cir. N.Y. 1897); and Smith v. Sun Print. & Pub. Assn., 55 F. 240 (2d Cir. N.Y. 1893). See also Burt v. Advertiser Newspaper Co., 28 N.E. 1, at 5 (1891).

46. Palmer v. New York News Pub. Co., 31 A.D. 210, at 212 (N.Y. App. Div. 1898). This reasoning adheres to the logic of Union Associated Press v. Press Pub. Co., 54 N.Y.S. 183 (N.Y. Sup. Ct. 1898) and Union Associated Press v. Heath, 63 N.Y.S. 96 (N.Y. App. Div.

1900), which held that wire services as well as the newspapers that used them could be considered independently as well as jointly liable for the publication of defamatory news.

47. Palmer v. New York News Pub. Co., 31 A.D. 210, at 213 (N.Y. App. Div. 1898), citing Morey v. Morning Journal Ass'n, 123 N.Y. 207 (N.Y. 1890).

48. Palmer v. Matthews, 29 A.D. 149 at 153 (N.Y. App. Div. 1898). "As has been well said by an eminent jurist, 'A party who seeks to testify in his own behalf must take the risk if there are vulnerable joints in his harness.'"

49. Palmer v. Matthews, 162 N.Y. 100 (N.Y. 1900).

50. Ibid., 102–3, citing Tillotson v. Cheetham, 3 Johns. 56 (N.Y. Sup. Ct. 1808); Palmer v. New York News Pub. Co., 31 A.D. 210 (N.Y. App. Div. 1898); Gray v. Brooklyn Union Pub. Co., 35 A.D. 286 (N.Y. App. Div. 1898); Morrison v. Press Pub. Co., 14 N.Y.S. 131 (N.Y. Super. Ct. 1891); Mattice v. Wilcox, 147 N.Y. 624 (N.Y. 1895); Hatfield v. Lasher, 81 N.Y. 246 (N.Y. 1880); Smith v. Sun Printing & Pub. Asso., 55 F. 240, at 245 (2d Cir. N.Y. 1893); Enquirer Co. v. Johnston, 72 F. 443 (7th Cir. Ind. 1896); Wilson v. Fitch, 41 Cal. 363, at 383 (Cal. 1871); and Sheahan v. Collins, 20 Ill. 325 (Ill. 1858).

## CHAPTER 5: THE OAKLEY CASES

1. See generally Shirl Kasper, *Annie Oakley* (Norman: University of Oklahoma Press, 1992), and Glenda Riley, *The Life and Legacy of Annie Oakley* (Norman: University of Oklahoma Press, 1994).

2. Louis Stotesbury, "The Famous 'Annie Oakley' Libel Suits," *American Printer* 40, no. 6 (August 1905): 533, 584–85.

3. Headline in *Cincinnati Post*, see Post Pub. Co. v. Butler, 137 F. 723 (6th Cir. Ohio 1905).

4. Kasper, *Annie Oakley*, 174–75.

5. Stotesbury, "The Famous 'Annie Oakley' Libel Suits."

6. Riley, *The Life and Legacy of Annie Oakley*, 75–76; Kasper, *Annie Oakley*, 112–13, 118.

7. *New York Press*, August 11, 1894, cited in Kasper, *Annie Oakley*, 118.

8. Kasper, *Annie Oakley*, 175, citing *Joliet* (Illinois) *Daily News*, October 3, 1906.

9. Letter to the editor from Frank Butler, *Forest and Stream*, April 30, 1910, 709.

10. This inexact figure is based on the list published in August 1905 in Stotesbury, "The Famous 'Annie Oakley' Libel Suits," the account of the case against a Chicago paper in *Forest and Stream*, October 10, 1906, 667, and on discussion of damage amounts in the twelve appellate opinions reviewed in this study.

11. Stotesbury, "The Famous 'Annie Oakley' Libel Suits," 584.

12. *Forest and Stream*, October 10, 1906, 667.

13. Stotesbury, "The Famous 'Annie Oakley' Libel Suits," 584.

14. "Oakley Damages Reduced," *Fourth Estate*, July 9, 1904, 3. See Post Pub. Co. v. Butler, 137 F. 723 (6th Cir. Ohio 1905).

15. Stotesbury, "The Famous 'Annie Oakley' Libel Suits," 584; see also "Mrs. Butler Wins One Libel Suit," *Fourth Estate,* March 26, 1904, 3.

16. Stotesbury, "The Famous 'Annie Oakley' Libel Suits," 583–84.

17. Butler v. Barret & Jordan, 130 F. 944, at 948–950 (C.C.D. Pa. 1904).

18. Ibid., at 950; see Morning Journal Asso. v. Rutherford, 51 F. 513 (2d Cir. N.Y. 1892).

19. Post Pub. Co. v. Butler, 137 F. 723, at 728 (6th Cir. Ohio 1905).

20. Butler v. Hoboken Printing & Publ'g Co., 73 N.J.L. 45, at 47 (Sup. Ct. 1905). The judge cited no case law or other authority.

21. Butler v. Gazette Co., 119 A.D. 767, at 773 (N.Y. App. Div. 1907), citing Smith v. Matthews, 152 N.Y. 152 (N.Y. 1897).

22. Butler v. Gazette Co., 119 A.D. 767, at 770 (N.Y. App. Div. 1907).

23. Ibid.

24. Ibid., citing Palmer v. N. Y. News Publishing Co., 31 A.D. 210 (N.Y. App. Div. 1898) and Palmer v. Matthews, 162 N.Y. 100 (N.Y. 1900) for the "well settled rule."

25. Butler v. Carter & R. Pub. Co., 135 F. 69, at 71 (5th Cir. Fla. 1905). Relatedly, the question before the 5th Circuit U.S. Court of Appeals in the case involving the *New Orleans Times-Democrat* was whether under Louisiana law Annie Oakley could sue for damages in her own name or Frank Butler had to bring the suit on her behalf. See Times-Democrat Pub. Co. v. Mozee, 136 F. 761 (5th Cir. La. 1905).

26. Butler v. Carter & R. Pub. Co., 135 F. 69, at 71–72 (5th Cir. Fla. 1905).

27. Butler v. Every Evening Printing Co., 140 F. 934, at 935 (C.C.D. Del. 1905).

28. Every Evening Printing Co. v. Butler, 144 F. 916 at 920 (3d Cir. Del. 1906).

29. Butler v. News-Leader Co., 104 Va. 1 (Va. 1905).

30. Kasper, *Annie Oakley,* 177, 180, citing six clippings from Oakley's scrapbook dated from 1904. Kasper wrote that in the years following the suits, Oakley's relationship with the press improved quickly.

31. Letter to the editor from Frank Butler, *Forest and Stream,* April 30, 1910, 709. According to biographer Glenda Riley, "Throughout the trials, an overwhelming number of Annie's fans, friends, sporting journal writers, shooters and other supporters sent her clippings and wrote letters of support" (*The Life and Legacy of Annie Oakley,* 79).

32. "To the Last Ditch," *Editor & Publisher,* January 23, 1904, 4. See also "Treatment of Certain Libel Cases by New York 'Press,'" *American Printer,* July 1905, 446.

33. "Treatment of Certain Libel Cases by New York 'Press,'" *American Printer,* July 1905, 446.

34. As of 1905, according to Stotesbury's report, the average settlement amount for the ten papers that agreed to them was about $800. The average award for the nine that went to trial was almost $2,200 ("The Famous 'Annie Oakley' Libel Suits," 533, 584–85).

35. "Mrs. Butler Wins One Libel Suit," *Fourth Estate,* March 26, 1904, 16.

36. Post Pub. Co. v. Butler, 137 F. 723, 725 (6th Cir. Ohio 1905).

## CHAPTER 6: BAD NEWS AND THE BAD TENDENCY TEST

1. According to Louis Stotesbury, the trial judge in Oakley's case against the *New Orleans Times-Democrat* reduced the jury's award from $7,500 to $5,000 ("The Famous 'Annie Oakley' Libel Suits," *American Printer* 40, no. 6 [August 1905]: 584). In the suit against the *Cincinnati Post*, the verdict was from $9,000 to $2,500. See Table 2 at the conclusion to chapter 5.

2. Oliver Wendell Holmes Jr., *The Common Law* (Boston: Little, Brown, 1881), 126.

3. Morning Journal Asso. v. Rutherford, 51 F. 513 (2d Cir. N.Y. 1892); Smith v. Sun Pub. Co., 50 F. 399 (C.C.D.N.Y. 1892); Smith v. Sun Printing & Pub. Asso., 55 F. 240 (2d Cir. N.Y. 1893); Smith v. Matthews, 27 N.Y.S. 120 (N.Y. Super. Ct. 1893); Smith v. Matthews, 46 N.E. 164 (1897); Palmer v. New York News Pub. Co., 31 A.D. 210 (N.Y. App. Div. 1898); Palmer v. Matthews, 162 N.Y. 100 (N.Y. 1900); Butler v. Barret & Jordan, 130 F. 944 (C.C.D. Pa. 1904); Post Pub. Co. v. Butler, 137 F. 723 (6th Cir. Ohio 1905); Butler v. Hoboken Printing & Publ'g Co., 73 N.J.L. 45 (Sup. Ct. 1905).

4. Smith v. Chicago Herald, *Chicago Legal News* 26, no. 40 (June 2, 1894): 317–18; Palmer v. Matthews, 29 A.D. 149 (N.Y. App. Div. 1898); Butler v. News-Leader Co., 104 Va. 1 (Va. 1905) (finding that the plaintiff, Annie Butler, was not identified in the story, which was about Annie Oakley); Butler v. Gazette Co., 119 A.D. 767 (N.Y. App. Div. 1907).

5. Smith v. Chicago Herald, 317–18. See the discussion of this case in chapter 3.

6. See discussion of evolving thinking about liability in tort law in chapter 2.

7. Palmer v. Matthews, 29 A.D. 149 (N.Y. App. Div. 1898). Two judges dissented in this decision, and it was later overturned in Palmer v. Matthews, 162 N.Y. 100 (N.Y. 1900).

8. Butler v. Gazette Co., 119 A.D. 767, at 773 (N.Y. App. Div. 1907).

9. See, for example, Smith v. Sun Pub. Co., 50 F. 399, at 402 (C.C.D.N.Y. 1892) (finding it reasonable to conclude that jury members found the newspapers' use of wire services to be "a wrong and perilous system"); Palmer v. New York News Pub. Co., 31 A.D. 210, at 216 (N.Y. App. Div. 1898) (arguing that "no charge could be made against [Palmer] that would be so destructive of his usefulness as the charge of dishonesty"); Post Pub. Co. v. Butler, 137 F. 723 at 728 (6th Cir. Ohio 1905) ("assuredly it was for the jury to say whether [publication of the story] did not evince a reckless and wanton disregard of the plaintiff's rights equivalent to an intentional violation of them").

10. Palmer v. Matthews, 29 A.D. 149 at 153 (N.Y. App. Div. 1898).

11. Palmer v. Matthews, 162 N.Y. 100 (N.Y. 1900).

12. The use of this term in libel law generally is discussed in chapter 2. In Palmer v. New York News Pub. Co., 31 A.D. 210, at 212 (N.Y. App. Div. 1898), Judge Rumsey made an analogy to an imaginary case where "100 persons at 100 different places make 100 separate publications of a libel in 100 different newspapers." In that instance, Rumsey said, the person libeled by the 100 newspapers could sue each publisher, and no single

defendant could "shelter himself behind the acts of the other 99, and say that 99/100 of the plaintiff's character was ruined by the others, and, therefore, he is liable for only 1/100 part of the damage."

13. Burt v. Advertiser Newspaper Co., 28 N.E. 1, at 5 (1891). See also Peck v. Tribune Co., 214 U.S. 185, 189–90 (1909), and discussion of Holmes and libel in chapter 2.

14. Dole v. Lyon, 10 Johns. 447 (N.Y. Sup. Ct. 1813).

15. Cooley, *Constitutional Limitations* (1868), 452–56.

16. Cooley, *Constitutional Limitations,* 5th ed. (Boston: Little, Brown, 1883), 562.

17. MacLean v. Scripps, 17 N.W. 815, at 818 (1884).

18. The research for this book did not include the whole of newspaper libel case law between 1890 and 1910, but its extensive review of contemporary cases, newspapers, trade publications, and other periodicals, as well as secondary literature on the topic of libel law, turned up almost zero instances of newspapers or publishers being forced out of business by a libel suit. See Norman Rosenberg, *Protecting the Best Men: An Interpretive History of the Law of Libel* (Chapel Hill: University of North Carolina Press, 1986), 198–99; Timothy Gleason, "The Libel Climate of the Late Nineteenth Century," *Journalism Quarterly* 70, no. 4 (1993).

19. See also Rosenberg, *Protecting the Best Men,* 199–200, for a discussion of libel law and self-censorship at the turn of the twentieth century more generally.

## CHAPTER 7: RETRACTION STATUTES

1. Post Pub. Co. v. Butler, 137 F. 723 (6th Cir. Ohio 1905); see 1900 Ohio Laws 295.

2. See Oh. Const. Art. I, § 16.

3. Post Pub. Co. v. Butler, 137 F. 723 at 727 (6th Cir. Ohio 1905).

4. 1885 Mich. Pub. Acts 233; 1887 Minn. Laws 308; 1895 Ind. Acts 91; 1895 Ill. Laws 315; 1897 Utah Laws 98; 1897 Wisc. Sess. Laws 640; 1897 Mass. Acts 561; 1897 Pa. Laws 204; 1898 N.J. Laws 476; 1898 Ala. Laws 32; 1899 Wash. Sess. Laws 101; 1900 Ohio Laws 295; 1901 Kans. Laws 439; 1901 N.C. Sess. Laws 784; 1903 Maine Acts 143; 1910 Ky. Acts 294; 1914 S.D. Laws 330. A few retraction statutes preceded the burst of seventeen studied here, including in Connecticut, Alabama, and Virginia. The United States grew from thirty-eight to forty-eight states between 1885 and 1912.

5. Several bills requiring that serial cases be consolidated into a single suit were proposed in the U.S. House and Senate between 1905 and 1910, and got some support from press associations, but none was passed. See "Publishers Urged to Act," *Fourth Estate,* December 24, 1904, 2; "A Bill to Protect Publishers in Libel Cases," *Los Angeles Times,* February 6, 1905; and "Oakley Suits Produce Bill to Stop Harvests," *Washington Times,* January 10, 1906, 9; "Bill Amending Law Favorably Reported to House," *New York Tribune,* January 16, 1909, 4. See also 39 Cong. Rec 1905, 144; 39 Cong. Rec. 1905, 87; 40

Cong. Rec. 1906, 501; 42 Cong. Rec. 1908, 402; 42 Cong. Rec. 1908, 3996; 41 Cong. Rec. 1907, 234; 45 Cong. Rec. 1910, 250.

6. Park v. Free Press Co., 40 N.W. 731 (1888); Hanson v. Krehbiel, 75 P. 1041 (1904); Osborn v. Leach, 47 S.E. 811 (1904); and Byers v. Meridian Printing Co., 95 N.E. 917 (1911); 1897 Ill. Laws 297; 1901 Pa. Laws 74.

7. Byers v. Meridian Printing Co. 95 N.E. 917 (1911).

8. Benjamin Briggs Herbert, *The First Decennium of the National Editorial Association of the United States* (Chicago: National Editorial Association, 1896), 77.

9. "Current Topics," *Albany Law Journal* 38 (July 7, 1888): 1.

10. American Newspaper Publishers Association, *Fourth Annual Convention of the American Newspaper Publishers Association* (1890): 21–27.

11. A. O. Bunnell, *Authorized History for Fifty Years: New York Press Association* (Dansville, NY: F.A. Owen Publishing, 1903), 52–53.

12. Herbert, *The First Decennium of the National Editorial Association of the United States,* 282–83; Bunnell, *Authorized History for Fifty Years,* 55.

13. Herbert, *The First Decennium of the National Editorial Association of the United States,* 544; *ANPA Convention Minutes,* n.p. (1895).

14. 1895 Ill. Laws 315 (approved June 24, 1895). The ANPA meeting was held in February 1895; the Indiana and Illinois statutes were passed later that year.

15. *ANPA Convention Minutes,* n.p. (1895).

16. Herbert, *The First Decennium of the National Editorial Association of the United States,* 544; *ANPA Convention Minutes,* n.p. (1895).

17. *ANPA Convention Minutes,* 23 and 27 (1890).

18. *ANPA Convention Minutes,* n.p. (1895).

19. Herbert, *The First Decennium of the National Editorial Association of the United States,* 282.

20. *ANPA Convention Minutes,* 24 (1890).

21. *ANPA Convention Minutes,* n.p. (1895).

22. *ANPA Convention Minutes,* 25 (1890).

23. Bunnell, *Authorized History for Fifty Years,* 58, 72, and 116. Worth noting is that Bunnell was editor of a country daily, the *Dansville* (New York) *Advertiser.*

24. Untitled Note, *Harvard Law Review* 3 (1889–90): 86.

25. American Bar Association, *Annual Meeting Minutes,* 194–95 (1895).

26. Herbert, *The First Decennium of the National Editorial Association of the United States,* 141–42.

27. National Editorial Association, *Official Proceedings of the Annual Convention,* 69–71 (1887).

28. Bunnell, *Authorized History for Fifty Years,* 52–53.

29. 1887 Minn. Laws 308; see Allen v. Pioneer Press Co., 40 Minn. 117 (1889).

30. 1887 Minn. Laws 308. Actual damages were defined as specified losses to "property, business, trade, profession or occupation."

31. Bunnell, *Authorized History for Fifty Years,* 55. Members would have prohibited lawyers from sharing damages awarded to a plaintiff.

32. *ANPA Convention Minutes,* 11 (1893).

33. *ILPC Convention Minutes* 29 (1895).

34. "Libels against Newsdealers," *Journalist,* March 22, 1884.

35. "The Editor and Libel," *Journalist,* July 30, 1898, 135.

36. "Vindicator Vindicated," *Newspaperdom,* March 18, 1897, 4.

37. "An Editorial Challenge," *Fourth Estate,* August 4, 1898, 4.

38. "The Past Year," *Fourth Estate,* January 6, 1898, 3.

39. "Illinois Modern Libel Law Repealed," *Fourth Estate,* June 10, 1897, 2.

40. Thomas Cooley, *A Treatise on The Law of Torts, or, the Wrongs Which Arise Independent of Contract,* 2nd ed. (Chicago: Callaghan, 1888), 93, 830.

41. Robert Gordon, "The Ideal and the Actual in the Law," in *The New High Priests: Lawyers in Post-Civil War America,* ed. Gerard Gawalt (Westport, CT: Greenwood Press, 1984), 54–57.

42. *ANPA Convention Minutes* 26 (1890). See 1885 Mich. Pub. Acts 233; Park v. Free Press Co., 40 N.W. 731 (1888).

43. Oliver Wendell Holmes Jr., *The Common Law* (Boston: Little, Brown, 1881), 110; Holmes, "Privilege, Malice, Intent," *Harvard Law Review* 8 (April 1894): 9.

44. "Libel Legislation"; *The Advocate* 1 (April 1, 1889): 145.

45. "Current Topics," *Albany Law Journal* 39 (April 13, 1889): 285.

46. "Current Topics," *Albany Law Journal* 47, 121 (February 18, 1893).

47. Ibid. See also Diane Borden, "Beyond Courtroom Victories: An Empirical and Historical Analysis of Women and the Law of Defamation" (Ph.D. diss., University of Washington, 1993). According to Borden, 43 of 130 reported defamation cases filed between 1897 and 1906 were brought by women. Borden argues that during this period "the courts, by compensating for the real harm to a woman's reputation, simultaneously reinforce[d] the cultural values that caused the harm in the first place." Borden found that women tended to win libel cases involving chastity or morality, which made up the vast majority of the lawsuits filed, but usually lost those involving "public-sphere roles," leading to the conclusion that law reinforced the "cultural assumption that women belong exclusively in the domestic realm and that their sexual virtue is their defining reputational trait."

48. "Current Topics," 47 *Albany Law Journal* 47 (February 18, 1893): 121.

49. "Notes," *American Law Review* 30 (March–April 1896): 276.

50. "Current Topics," *Albany Law Journal* 55 (March 27, 1897): 194.

51. "Current Topics," *Albany Law Journal* 56 (July 10, 1897): 20.

52. 1895 Ind. Acts 91; 1895 Ill. Laws 315; 1897 Utah Laws 98; 1897 Wisc. Sess. Laws

640; 1897 Mass. Acts 561; 1897 Pa. Laws 204; 1898 N.J. Laws 476; 1898 Ala. Laws 32; 1899 Wash. Sess. Laws 101; 1900 Ohio Laws 295; 1901 Kans. Laws 439; 1901 N.C. Sess. Laws 784; 1903 Maine Acts 143.

53. 1885 Mich. Pub. Acts 233; 1887 Minn. Laws 308.

54. 1910 Ky. Acts 294; 1914 S.D. Laws 330.

55. Park v. Free Press Co., 40 N.W. 731 (1888).

56. Allen v. Pioneer Press Co., 40 Minn. 117 (1889).

57. Hanson v. Krehbiel, 75 P. 1041 (1904); Osborn v. Leach, 47 S.E. 811 (1904).

58. Byers v. Meridian Printing Co. 95 N.E. 917 (1911).

59. 1887 Minn. Laws 308; 1898 Ala. Laws 32; 1899 Wash. Sess. Laws 101; 1901 Kans. Laws 439; 1901 N.C. Sess. Laws 784; and 1914 S.D. Laws 330.

60. 1885 Mich. Pub. Acts 233; 1887 Minn. Laws 308; 1895 Ind. Acts 91; 1895 Ill. Laws 315; 1897 Utah Laws 98; 1897 Wisc. Sess. Laws 640; Wash. Sess. Laws 101; 1901 Kans. Laws 439; 1901 N.C. Sess. Laws 784; 1914 S.D. Laws 330.

61. 1898 N.J. Laws 476 applied to newspapers, magazines, publications, periodicals, or serials; 1910 Ky. Acts 294 included newspapers and publications.

62. 1898 Ala. Laws 32. Any defendant could mitigate damages through a retraction or evidence that the libel was accidental; plaintiffs suing newspapers were required to serve notice five days in advance of the lawsuit. When newspapers made a retraction, plaintiffs could recover only actual damages.

63. 1897 Mass. Acts 561; 1897 Pa. Laws 204; 1900 Ohio Laws 295; 1903 Maine Acts 143.

64. 1897 Wisc. Sess. Laws 640; 1897 Pa. Laws 204; 1899 Wash. Sess. Laws 101.

65. 1897 Wisc. Sess. Laws 640. This is commonly known as the "neutral reportage" privilege. See "Libel and Slander: Construction and Application of the Neutral Reportage Privilege," *American Law Reports* 13, no. 6 (2016): 111.

66. 1897 Pa. Laws 204. In 1901, the Pennsylvania Legislature repealed this statute. 1901 Pa. Laws 74. In 1903, the state legislature passed an anti-press reform bill, which Governor Samuel Pennypacker wrote in a signing statement was intended to address "widespread dissatisfaction" with newspapers. See 1903 Pa. Laws 349. In 1907, four months after Pennypacker left office, the 1903 law was repealed. See 1907 Pa. Laws 126. See Steven Piott, "The Right of the Cartoonist: Samuel Pennypacker and Freedom of the Press," *Pennsylvania History: A Journal of Mid-Atlantic Studies* 55, no. 2 (1988): 78.

67. 1887 Minn. Laws 308; 1895 Ind. Acts 91; 1895 Ill. Laws 315; 1897 Utah Laws 98; 1901 Kans. Laws 439; 1914 S.D. Laws 330.

68. *Annual Report of the American Bar Association* (1896): 216–17.

69. Park v. Free Press Co., 40 N.W. 731, 734–35 (1888).

70. Allen v. Pioneer Press Co., 40 Minn. 117–20 (1889).

71. Osborn v. Leach, 47 S.E. 811, at 815 (1904). One member of the court disagreed with his brethren on this point: "While concurring in the result, I feel constrained to say that, in my opinion, the so-called libel act is unconstitutional, inasmuch as it dis-

criminates between the editor of a newspaper and the ordinary citizen" (Douglas, J. concurring).

72. Post Pub. Co. v. Butler, 137 F. 723 at 727 (6th Cir. Ohio 1905).

73. See Hanson v. Krehbiel, 75 P. 1041, at 1043 (1904); Osborn v. Leach, 47 S.E. 811, at 814–15 (1904); and Byers v. Meridian Printing Co. 95 N.E. 917, at 919–20 (1911), and "Current Topics," *Albany Law Journal* 47 (February 18, 1893): 121.

74. Park v. Free Press Co., 40 N.W. 731, at 733 (1888). It is worth noting that several retraction statutes that passed after *Park* appear to have paid some heed to Campbell's concerns by specifically stating that they did not apply to libels of women. See 1895 Ind. Acts 91; 1901 Kans. Laws 439; and 1914 S.D. Laws 330.

75. Park v. Free Press Co., 40 N.W. 731, at 733 (1888).

76. See 1895 Ind. Acts 91; 1901 Kans. Laws 439; 1914 S.D. Laws 330.

77. Hanson v. Krehbiel, 75 P. 1041 (1904); Osborn v. Leach, 47 S.E. 811 (1904); Byers v. Meridian Printing Co. 95 N.E. 917 (1911).

78. Allen v. Pioneer Press Co., 40 Minn. 117, 123–24 (1889).

79. Code of Ala. § 6–5–184 to 188; Ariz. Rev. Stat. § 12–653.01 to 12–653.05; Cal. Civ. Code § 48a; Conn. Gen. Stat. § 52–237; Fla. Stat. § 770.02; Ga. Code Ann. § 51–5–11 to 51–5–12; Idaho Code § 6–712; Ind. Code Ann. § 34–15–3–3; Iowa Code § 659.2 to 659.3; Ky. Rev. Stat. § 411.051, 411.061; 14 Maine Rev. Stat. § 153; Mass. Ann. Laws chap. 231 § 93; Mich. Stat. Ann. § 600.2911; Minn. Stat. § 548.06; Miss. Code Ann. § 95–1–5; Mont. Code Ann. § 27–1–818 to 27–1–821; Neb. Rev. Stat. § 25–840.01; Nev. Rev. Stat. Ann. § 41.336 to 41.338; N.J. Stat. § 2A:43–2; N.C. Gen. Stat. § 99–2; N.D. Cent. Code, § 32–43–02 to 32–43–10; Ohio Rev. Code Ann. § 2739.03, 2739.13, and 2739.14; Okla. Stat. Ann. Tit. 12 § 1446a; Or. Rev. Stat. Ann. § 31.210, 31.215, and 31.220; S.D. Codified Laws § 20–11–6 to 20–11–6; Tenn. Code Ann. § 29–24–103; Tex. Civ. Prac. & Rem. Code § 73.003; Utah Code Ann. § 45–2–1; Va. Code Ann. § 8.01–48; W. Va. Code § 57–2–4; Wisc. Stat. § 895.05. This includes nine of the statutes discussed here: in Alabama, Indiana, Kentucky, Maine, Massachusetts, New Jersey, South Dakota, Utah, and Wisconsin.

80. Primary and secondary sources cite Layne v. Tribune Co., 108 Fla. 177 (1933) as the first time the wire service defense was recognized. I argue that the serial libel cases show some judges were willing to accept it earlier. See Kyu Ho Youm, "The 'Wire Service' Libel Defense," *Journalism Quarterly* 70, no. 3 (1993); Jennifer Del Medico, "Are Talebearers Really as Bad as Talemakers? Rethinking Republisher Liability in an Information Age," *Fordham Urban Law Journal* 31 (2004): 1409; Daxton R. Stewart, "When Retweets Attack: Are Twitter Users Liable for Republishing the Defamatory Tweets of Others?" *Journalism and Mass Communication Quarterly* 90, no. 2 (2013). Courts began to recognize a "single publication rule," under which a plaintiff cannot sue the same publisher more than once for the same article and can only receive damages once for a single libelous article regardless of how often it is republished elsewhere, in the 1940s. The single publication rule was recognized in Hartmann v. Time, Inc., 166 F.2d 12

(3d Cir. 1947) cert denied 334 U.S. 838 (1948). In 1952, a Uniform Single Publication Act was drafted by the National Conference of Commissioners on Uniform State Laws in 1952, and appears in *Restatement 2d of Torts*, "Single and Multiple Publications" (1977), § 577A. Most states have adopted the rule through legislation or court recognition. See Stewart, "When Retweets Attack," 237; and Sapna Kumar, "Comment: Website Libel and the Single Publication Rule," *University of Chicago Law Review* 70 (2013): 639, 642–43.

81. New York Times v. Sullivan, 376 U.S. 254, at 273 (1964).

## CONCLUSION

1. Smith v. Chicago Herald, *Chicago Legal News* 26, no. 40 (June 2, 1894): 317; see also Cooley, *Constitutional Limitations* (1868): 452–56.

2. See Clifton Lawhorne, *Defamation and Public Officials: The Evolving Law of Libel* (Carbondale: Southern Illinois University Press, 1971); W. Wat Hopkins, *Actual Malice: Twenty-Five Years after Times v. Sullivan* (New York: Praeger, 1989); and Norman Rosenberg, *Protecting the Best Men: An Interpretive History of the Law of Libel* (Chapel Hill: University of North Carolina Press, 1986).

3. New York Times v. Sullivan 376 U.S. 254 at 270 (1964).

4. Patrick File, "Retract, Expand: Libel Law, The Professionalization of Journalism, and the Limits of Press Freedom at the Turn of the Twentieth Century," *Communication Law and Policy* 22 (2017): 275–308; Eric Easton, *Mobilizing the Press: Defending the First Amendment in the Supreme Court* (Lake Mary, FL: Vandeplas Publishing, 2012); Dean C. Smith, "The Real Story behind the Nation's First Shield Law: Maryland, 1894–1897," *Communication Law & Policy* 19, no. 3 (2014): Emily Erickson, "The Watchdog Joins the Fray: The Press, Records Audits, and State Access Reform," *Journalism & Comm. Monographs* 16 (2014): 104–54; Michael Schudson, *The Rise of the Right to Know: Politics and the Culture of Transparency, 1945–1975* (Cambridge, MA: Harvard University Press, 2015).

5. This is in keeping with the findings of David Rabban and others that during the late nineteenth and early twentieth century, important thinking about free speech was prevalent in various legal conflicts but legal discourse rarely offered direct or explicit interpretations of the free speech rights enshrined in the First Amendment or state constitutions. See David Rabban, *Free Speech in Its Forgotten Years* (New York: Cambridge University Press, 1997).

6. U.S. Constitution, Amendment I; in pertinent part: "Congress shall make no law . . . abridging the freedom of speech, or of the press." See, for example, Potter Stewart, "Or of the Press," *Hastings Law Journal* 26 (1975): 631–37; Anthony Lewis, "A Preferred Position for Journalism?," *Hofstra Law Review* 7 (1979): 595–627; and David A. Anderson, "Freedom of the Press," *Texas Law Review* 80 (2002): 429–530. Most recently, the Court

has stirred debate by dividing on whether an exception for news media in federal campaign finance law was constitutional in *Citizens United v. FEC,* 558 U.S. 310 (2010). See Sonja R. West, "The Press, Then & Now," *Ohio State Law Review* 77 (2016): 56.

7. Eugene Volokh, "Freedom for the Press as an Industry, or Freedom for the Press as a Technology? From the Framing to Today," *University of Pennsylvania Law Review* 160 (2011): 459–540.

8. West, "The Press, Then & Now," and "Awakening the Press Clause," *UCLA Law Review* 58 (2011): 1025–70.

9. Scott Gant, *We're All Journalists Now: The Transformation of the Press and Reshaping of the Law in the Internet Age* (New York: Simon and Schuster, 2007); see also Dan Gillmor, *We the Media: Grassroots Media by the People, For the People* (Sebastopol, CA: O'Reilly Media, 2006); and Clay Shirky, *Here Comes Everybody: The Power of Organizing without Organizations* (London: Penguin, 2008).

10. 521 U.S. 844 (1997).

11. Communications Decency Act of 1996, 47 U.S.C. § 230(c)(1). In relevant part: "No provider or user of an interactive computer service shall be treated as the publisher or speaker of any information provided by another information content provider."

12. Daxton R. Stewart, "When Retweets Attack: Are Twitter Users Liable for Republishing the Defamatory Tweets of Others?" *Journalism and Mass Communication Quarterly* 90, no. 2 (2013); Adeline Allen, "Twibel Retweeted: Twitter and the Single Publication Rule," *Journal of High Technology and Law* 15 (2014): 63–96.

13. David Ardia, "Free Speech Savior or Shield for Scoundrels: An Empirical Study of Intermediary Immunity under Section 230 of the Communications Decency Act," *Loyola of Los Angeles Law Review* 43, no. 2 (2010): 373–506, 411.

14. Jeffrey Blevins, "OPINION: Court Decision Cautions Us to Care for the Truth," Cincinnati.com, August 3, 2013.

15. Jess Bravin, "Amid All the Talk, a Willingness to Curb Some Speech," *Wall Street Journal,* July 1, 2010, A4.

# *INDEX*

*t* indicates a table

PATRICK C. FILE is assistant professor of media law at the Reynolds School of Journalism at the University of Nevada, Reno, where his research, public engagement, and teaching focus on helping us better understand how we define and regulate journalism at the intersection of law, technology, and professional practices. Prior to his academic career, File won national awards as a student journalist at Simpson College in Indianola, Iowa; worked for his hometown newspaper in Mount Pleasant, Iowa; and reported for publications in Iowa and upstate New York. He holds a doctorate and a master's degree from the University of Minnesota School of Journalism and Mass Communication.

Cazenovia Public Library
0003201560426